MW00716454

WHAT'S LEFT?

The New Democratic Party in Renewal

WHAT'S LEFT?

The New Democratic Party in Renewal

EDITED BY Z. DAVID BERLIN
AND HOWARD ASTER

mosaic press

National Library of Canada Cataloguing in Publication Data

Berlin Z. David, 1951-
    What's left? : the New Democratic Party in renewal

ISBN 0-88962-779-7

    1. New Democratic Party.   I. Aster, Howard   II. Title

JL197.N4B47 2001   324.27107   C2001-903211-0

No part of this book may be reproduced or transmitted electronically in any for, by any means, electronic or mechanical, including photocopying and recording, information storage ands retrieval systems, without permission in writing from the publisher, except a reviewer who may quote brief passages in a review.

Published by Mosaic Press, offices and warehouse at 1252 Speers Rd., Units 1 & 2, Oakville, ON L6L 5N9, Canada and Moaic Press, PMB 145, 4500 Witmer Industrial Estates, Niagara Falls, NY, 14305-1386, USA

Mosaic Press acknowledges the assistance of the Canada Council and the Department of Canadian Heritage, Government of Canada for their support of our publishing programme.

Copyright © 2001, the Authors
Printed and bound in Canada
ISBN 0-88962-779-7

MOSAIC PRESS, in Canada:
1252 Speers Road, Units 1 & 2,
Oakville, Ontario
L6L 5N9
Phone/Fax: 905-825-2130
mosaicpress@on.aibn.com

MOSAIC PRESS, in U.S.A.:
4500 Witmer Industrial Estates
PMB 145, Niagara Falls, NY
14305-1386
Phone/Fax: 1-800-387-8992
mosaicpress@on.aibn.com

Le Conseil des Arts   The Canada Council
du Canada   for the Arts

Acknowledgements

The Editors would like to thank all the Contributors to this volume. Thanks to Sylvia Nickerson for her devotion to the project and her design skills.

We would especially like to acknowledge the support of the David Lewis Trust through which wide distribution of this volume has been assured.

The Contributors

EARL BERGER is Associate Director, Policy at the Hay Health Care Consulting Group and managing director of the semi-annual national survey, The Berger Population Health Monitor.

JORDAN BERGER works for OPSEU and a federal New Democratic Party candidate in the Davenport riding, Toronto.

EDWARD BROADBENT is former national leader of the New Democratic Party. He has been on the faculty of various universities, including York University, Oxford University and most recently, Carleton University.

GERALD CAPLAN is the former federal Secretary for the New Democratic Party and a long-time strategic advisor for the NDP at both the provincial and federal levels.

PIERRE DUCASSE is the co-ordinator of Table nationale des Corporations de developpement communautaire du Quebec.

SHOLOM GLOUBERMAN is President of Health and Everything and works at the Baycrest Centre for Geriatric Care.

ANDREW JACKSON is Director of Research for the Canadian Council on Social Development.

DAVID LANGILLE is Director of Research at the Centre for Social Justice.

ROBERT MACDERMID is a member of the Political Science Department at York University and has written numerous articles on campaign and party financing.

ALEXA MCDONOUGH is National Leader of the New Democratic Party.

HENRY MILNER is a member of the Department of Political Science at Concordia University and has written extensively on social democracy in Sweden.

JIM STANFORD is an economist for the Canadian Auto Workers union and Sven Robinson is the New Democratic Party MM for Burnaby, B.C.

MICHAEL VALPY is journalist, a member of the editorial board and national political columnist for the Globe and Mail and a former federal candidate for the NDP.

CHRIS WATSON is a Director of Research for the New Democratic Party at Queen's Park, Provincial Legislature, Toronto.

ARMINE YALNIZYAN is an economist and a member of the New Democratic Party Steering Committee on renewal.

MARCH ZWELLING is President of Vector Research + Development Inc.

Table of Contents

Three: What's Left? Public Policy and the New Democratic Party

Foreword

Z. DAVID BERLIN

THE IDEA FOR THIS VOLUME FIRST CAME INTO BEING at the May 2001 conference on social democracy sponsored by the McGill Institute for the Study of Canada. It was directly following a particularly stressful two hour panel discussion in which John Richards tested the assembly's commitment to civility, that it suddenly struck several of us that something real was going on; that a historical moment was being constituted and that it needed to be documented. The very fact that it struck us and that no one struck John Richards seemed itself worthy of a book or two. I say this only half jokingly.

To me it appeared as though a new maturity was settling in and that it was dislodging the youthful idealism of our incipient spirit. Participants at the Montreal conference, party members at the Toronto conference on Renewal and throughout the renewal process were doing their utmost to curb the impulse to punch the next fellow in the nose. There was a lot of intense listening going on. Partisans suddenly seemed willing to resist the quick fix. They were passing on the timeworn cliché (I didn't hear one round of " shame… shame") and the ubiquitous social policy began looking like a thing of the past.

These sorts of maturities strike at the heart of the matter put forward in this collection. What is the matter? The central question of this volume pertains to the tension between principle and pragmatism, between a party of principle which many social democrats think of as the NDP and a pragmatic party which is the big, one–stop-shop party in Canada.

Stripped of partisan bombast, pragmatism refers to the here and now, to the immediate, to the oiler and to the oil that stops a shoe from squeaking. Principle refers to the long view, to the seven league boots that the Left represents. It is interesting to trace the way in which the idea of principle gets articulated by the various contributors. In most cases the sensitive analyst will find that the concept is updated and rendered fit for a party that even as it undergoes rebirth, is still very much a mature entity.

Judging from these contributions, social democrats are for the most part no longer hotheads — no longer cloistered romantics and impatient Stalinists. Their viewpoint on politics in general and on social policy in particular is much more tempered and much more thoughtful than was the case in the recent past. Social democrats in Canada are willing to debate core issues. Bernstein's idea of the market as a neutral thing that needs to be governed but not transcended seems to hold much more sway than it did in the past.

For those readers who are willing to read between the lines the current response to the question "what makes us social democrats" is also addressed in this volume. In the first instance the principle assumptions of social democracy are articulated as well as ever in Ed Broadbent's piece entitled "Social Democracy in Theory and Practice". But the spirit of the response to the question of " who we are" is not confined to that seminal essay. Where once this response would have entailed a turn to the creator and to nature — "it is an overflow of social conscience" or we are those with a deficiency of Hobbesian testosterone" — these days most social democrats confess to having made a choice. To choose social democracy over say, liberalism is to remain focussed on the big picture, to opt for the sustainable, the livable, a measure of substantive equality etc. From this ultimate choice everything else follows.

Another recent development is worth noting. With very few exceptions, contributors to this volume counsel the party to reorganize itself and seek power rather than mere influence of the political agenda. Given the history of the NDP this may seem a rather abstract recommendation and Gerry Caplan in his essay entitled "The Truth Shall Make You Third" says just that. The point I think Gerry misses has to do with the power of principle itself. When it is allowed free reign a principle works to unleash and focus the imagination which for its part releases seretonin or whatever else you want to call the juice that gets creativity underway. This is the pragmatic side of principle. And it works.

Here are some examples culled from the essays in this volume. In a piece entitled "Rethinking The Principles in Health Care Reform" Earl Berger reminds us that even as we remain resolved to uphold the 5 principles of Canada's Health Act " there is much more room to manouevre and many more areas in which to be creative" than is commonly believed. To put forward a platform that simply pours more money into an expanded Health Care is to do nothing more than declare and re declare ad nauseum that we represent the principle .

There are many ways of skinning the cat, Berger tells us. For example: in order to alleviate the shortages of physicians, a political party might challenge the Colleges restrictions upon foreign physician licensing. Berger is not suggesting that we relax our standards but that we jettison all that is merely exclusionary and protective about these standards. To be sure this sort of risk is not the kind of risk one could expect a liberal party to take. It is a natural for social democrats who have a greater sense of ownership over the health care system. It is after all, their baby.

The same sort of creativity is displayed in many of the essays. Armine Yelnizian, to take but one more example, calls for a new language for social democracy. This call is particularly relevant in the aftermath of the September 11, massacres. Unfortunately it took a crisis to silence the clarion call to reduce taxes. Unfortunately it took a horror to remind people of the importance of government leadership and yes, sovereignty. It is unlikely that the Right will be able to resist military reaction for very long. After all that is the immediate, the here and now, (can I say, the short-sighted view?). It falls to the Left to put forward their own brand of leadership and to express it in a new language created for these times and this context. "Culture as the first line of natural defense" works in principle.

Toronto, ON
October 2001

Introduction

HOWARD ASTER

IN MOST WESTERN DEMOCRATIC SOCIETIES TODAY, public institutions are under increasing stress and pressure. Assaults are coming from all sides. Technological change produces many dislocations; financial pressures are abundant; public cynicism and apathy erode support and trust in democratic governments; the balance between the public good and the private good is being questioned; the very nature of civil society itself is under close scrutiny; fear and terror appear to be nibbling at any pretense of political stability and a global order. In Canada, our public institutions are not immune to such difficulties. Even political parties, as part of the structure of our public institutions, are experiencing times of dramatic turmoil and transformation. The New Democratic Party presently finds itself in the throes of intense agitation. The times demand the Party and its members embark on an earnest, at times painful questioning of the past, while daring venture a look to the future.

Let us remember, however, that Canadian political experience the last century has given us some simple, but profoundly true, rules or even laws of our political party life. What are they?

1) volatility
2) generational transformations lead to party shakeups
3) all political parties undergo periods of ascendancy and decline
4) we, in Canada, live with a three plus party system
5) the ideological spectrum in Canada is wider and more vibrant than in the United States.

Aristotle argues that everything, both in the natural and social world, undergoes a process of development and decay. The question that appears to face the NDP today is whether its contemporary experience denotes a process of terminal decay or can there be a process of regeneration?

The essays in this book give us some insight into the conditions and likely directions for the New Democratic Party in Canada over the next generation.

The book is divided into three parts. The first part locates the New Democratic Party within the larger context of social democracy. The essay by Edward Broadbent relocates the discourse on social democracy in a larger comparative, historical and theoretical context. The other essays by David Langille, Andrew Jackson, Armine Yalnizyan and Michael Valpy remind us that the discourse on social democracy should be looked at in a comparative manner and with a sensitivity to the language of social democracy and the media.

The second part exposes the internal debates that are taking place within the New Democratic Party as a functioning political party in Canada today. The debate is open, it is fierce, it is extremely self-critical. One of the most important conclusions to emerge from this debate is that there needs to be, or more precisely, there must be, a political party which is value-driven and expresses the significant social democratic value system which is so deeply lodged in the Canadian public. As a number of essays assert, Canadians embrace social democratic values in very large numbers, but they do not seem to vote as social democrats. That is the challenge.

The third part of this volume explores a number of very important public policy issues which a revitalized NDP ought to address, such as public education, health policy, urban issues, political finance. No doubt, there are many others. What emerges is that the search for a distinctively social democratic take on public policy issues is requires in order for there to be reverberations in the Canadian electorate.

The logic of the organization of this volume is rather simple. Any political party, not just the NDP, must begin with a clarification of its fundamental value system, or ideology. Times change and value systems redefine themselves based upon historical circumstance and global transformations. Neo-liberalism, neo-conservatism are just two fairly recent efforts at ideological adaptation and re-invention. Social democrats last re-invented themselves in Canada some forty years ago. Today, we may well be at a cusp in our history where Canadian social democrats will re-invent themselves again.

Political parties, however, are not just vehicles for value systems and ideologies, they are also fighting machines, electoral beasts, instruments in the struggle for political power. In Canada, our history and our heritage teaches us that parties come and go, that our party system is quite fluid and the Canadian electorate likes novelty, fluidity and the unexpected. Electoral success and failure tends to be almost volcanic! Look what happened to the Progressive Conservative Party not more than ten years ago. Look what happened to the Liberal Party of Canada – the 'government party – not more than twenty years ago. Look what happened to the Social Credit Party! Look what happened to the Progressive Party!

Electoral defeat is a very vengeful process in Canada. From a distance, it appears that the Canadian electorate is a fiercely unforgiving electorate. We are quite content to create new parties and to re-create old ones. This Canadian pattern is significantly different from the United States and also the UK.

So what is to be done about the NDP, or what will the NDP do to itself? And, after that, what will be the judgement of the Canadian electorate? Parties are about ideas, process and policy. If we look at these three components, as exposed in this volume, while there may be a lot of debate within the NDP, there also appears to be a discernible core on all three fronts. The public judgement at the federal level on the re-invention or the renewal of the NDP will be carried out within three years.

Oakville, ON
October 2001

ONE:

WHAT'S LEFT?
Social Democracy in Perspective

Social Democracy In Theory and Practice — The Way Ahead[1]

EDWARD BROADBENT

CANADA DOES NOT NEED ANOTHER LIBERAL PARTY. Nor does it require, in this era of right-of-centre politics, a party comprised of good-to-be-in-permanent-opposition self-described "radicals." It needs a re-invigorated New Democratic Party that is confident about the relevance of social democracy to the well being of the majority of Canadians. Today, most of the governments in western Continental Europe are social democratic; a distinct type of politics and society responsible for transforming the lives of millions of ordinary people. These countries have tough-minded governments who preside over market economies and understand that there must be an emphasis on substantive equality if liberty is to be an equitably experienced aspect of democratic citizenship. What Canada's Liberals and the "radicals" have in common is a rejection of social democracy. The former have no commitment to substantive equality. And the latter have nothing but disdain for markets.[2]

Looking at the past decade, we can see that when it comes to social justice, ideology matters and governments count. While Canada, Britain and the United States went one way during this period, social democrats went another. Changes in the economies of all OECD countries, resulting from technical innovation and globalization, widened the market-income and wealth gap between classes and regions. Continental European governments responded by looking for ways to extend the social charter and by becoming economically more efficient. In contrast, Canadian, British and American governments slashed social programs and deepened inequality. The Danes and the Dutch introduced globally competitive labour market flexibility without cutting back on social benefits or rights of their workers. And while market-produced levels of child poverty in Sweden and Canada were virtually identical during this period (around 24%), after government intervention only 2.6% of Swedish kids remained in poverty whereas in Canada, the percentage was six-times greater – and in Britain and United States the situation was even worse. (Five continental European countries almost eliminated child poverty as the numbers in Canada continued to grow). And while Britain, Canada and the United States stood back and watched profitable companies lay off workers, the French government responded to such action with measures to strengthen the rights of workers and tax changes which will penalize profitable companies if they seek greater profitability by even more layoffs. While the rich in Germany, Sweden and the Netherlands continue to send their children to the well-funded public schools attended by everyone else, our wealthiest province has embarked upon a two-class system of education already firmly entrenched in the United States and Britain. And in the same three European countries, productivity increases, averaged over the period, equalled that of the United States. In sum, continental European social democracies see social justice and economic efficiency not in competition, but as complementary components of national policy. They also understand that liberty and equality should be seen, not in conflict, but as mutually reinforcing.

How did this come about? Social democracy took off during the post-World War II years, a by-product of strong unions and social solidarity fostered by the war. Democratic citizens were determined to build a new social order, one that would combine social

3

and economic justice with our liberal political institutions. The goal was to ensure that all citizens were equally entitled to a range of universal social rights. These would not be allocated on the basis of the market but provided as rights of citizenship. It was understood that market economies were required to generate the necessary wealth for these new egalitarian social rights.

However, it was also understood that for this to happen, a market economy required an intervening government. This combination – social rights, market economy, and activist government – laid a strong foundation in Europe for what was neither Marxist, nor liberal, but rather a novel, expanded notion of democratic citizenship. Social democrats there and in Canada contended that such societies could achieve a much higher level of personal freedom and distributive justice than had ever been thought possible. This notion of the need for deeply embedded social rights, alongside the operations of the market economy, is unique to social democracy.

Modern liberals have a deeply embedded and unresolved conflict. On the one hand, they would agree that the goal of a tolerant, open society should be to ensure that all human beings have the equal right to the development of their talents and interests. At the same time, they remain wedded to the ethic of the market place: economic rewards should be allocated on the principle of greater amounts going to those with greater innate ability *or* to those who make a more energetic effort *or* who perform a task that the market values. Assuming the existence of laws to stop the formation of cartels and government guarantees to ensure that no person or family remains in abject poverty, according to this ethic, any resulting inequalities are exactly as they should be.

Although any such market system entails serious material inequalities at birth, for the modern liberal, equal access to education or post-industrial skills training should make it possible for all individuals to compete more or less equally. In terms of rights, what citizens need are only equal civil and political rights. It's using these rights politically and in the economy that will lead to the justified material inequalities produced by the market. Seen by a modern liberal who accepts the ethic of the market place, a "just society" that also includes social and economic rights would be an oxymoron. This is because such rights, by definition, alter significantly the distribution results of the market.

Instead of egalitarian social and economic rights of citizenship, liberals prefer "safety-net" welfare. While preserving other serious inequalities, this is intended (in principle) to ensure that no one is destitute. Jean Chrétien does not proclaim the need for a range of social rights for all. Instead, he justifies Liberal social policy by asserting, "governments must help those who cannot help themselves." Canada's other conservative parties who remain equally wedded to the market-ethic strongly agree.

Social democrats differ from other Canadians on precisely this issue. Like the modern liberal, we see the goal as each citizen having the equal right to develop his or her talents and to participate equally in shaping political decisions. However, when we talk about equality, we do not take this to mean simply equality before the law, or the equal right to participate in politics, or the equal formal entitlement to have access to employment, or gender and sexual equality, or the freedom to purchase goods and services in the marketplace. Social democrats believe in all these rights, but more as well.

For us the degree of substantive equality in society matters a great deal if the equal right to development is to exist. And it is in this context that we see equality and freedom to be inextricably connected. To act freely is to make choices. In any society that lacks a significant degree of material equality, we see it as self-evident that the capacity to act freely is also unequal. In a market economy, most goods and services are bought and sold. Whether for baseball games, food on the table, music lessons, kids' clothing, or a holiday – to exercise free choice requires cash. The less cash, the less choice; the less choice the less freedom. Rich families not only have more money, they have more freedom. Citizenship is unequal.

We social democrats therefore, reject the market mechanism as the means for ensuring an equitable distribution of the wealth of a nation. It is inherently unfair. Nor do we accept as adequate, measures intended to achieve only equality of opportunity. We strongly assert that democracy's goal of equal and participatory citizenship can only be achieved by government measures designed to provide more real equality. Only combining progressive taxation with social rights that remove many goods and services entirely from market criteria can do this. Only by becoming social democratic in shaping market outcomes can the liberal goal of the equal right of all to full human development take place.

MARKETS: HARNESSED AND SUBVERTED

To social democrats, the prospect of ever-increasing social equality necessarily involves a complex set of relationships that serve to both harness and subvert the power of the market. They see the process of democracy as the most effective means of ensuring that men and women do not become enslaved to the severe inequality and commercialization of life that results from unfettered markets. While they see the innovative efficiency of markets as the best means of ensuring the production, distribution and sale of most goods and services, social democrats believe that certain goods, services and activities are so important that they should be ensured as a matter of right to all citizens. And, to achieve democracy's objective of participatory citizenship, social democrats seek means to make both the corporate and public sectors more responsive and accountable to workers and citizens.

By ensuring that the negative results of market forces are effectively countered by non-market social rights and other government action in selective parts of the economy, in the arts and the environment, continental European social democrats have managed to *retain the benefits of market economies without becoming market societies.* Progressive taxation *and* the strong presence of social and economic rights that ensure major elements of equality for all citizens in the essentials of personal and family life can considerably reduce the negative effects of market-based inequalities. Put in terms appropriate to our age, as long as ordinary citizens can send their children to good public schools, have free comprehensive health services, benefit from income and retraining programs when they are unemployed, buy a computer, have an annual paid vacation with access to healthy air and clean beaches, and retire with dignity, most will regard with neither envy nor contempt the existence of an affluent few. They will simply want to get on with their own lives.

It is the presence of strong, universal social rights – whose specific content varies over time – that has made possible the sense of freedom and social equality experienced by millions of ordinary people. Free from the time demands and anxiety otherwise needed to make personal market decisions about health, pensions, child care, and university education, citizens in established social democracies are literally freer to choose how to spend their time: listening to Bach, playing soccer, or drinking beer and talking with friends on a sunny afternoon.

By drawing upon our own history, Canadian social democrats can find a rich source of ideas that can inspire us in the building of such a society. It was a Canadian social democrat who first drew together the amalgam of secular and religious values which subsequently emerged in 1948 as the Universal Declaration of Human Rights. John Humphrey, a professor of law at McGill University, became the world's first public servant with a human rights mandate. Invited to go to the United Nations to serve a committee chaired by Eleanor Roosevelt, he produced the first draft of the Universal Declaration. Taken along with its companions, the Covenant on Economic Social and Cultural Rights and the Covenant on Civil and Political Rights, the result constitutes a deeply social democratic global objective.

—Instead of seeing liberty and equality in conflict, these values are correctly understood to be mutually reinforcing. Instead of seeing individuals as permanently in competition with each other, they are portrayed as members of communities with obligations as well as rights. At the outset of all three documents there is the important recognition of the importance of equality. All men and women are seen to have an equal claim to a life of dignity *and* an equal claim to the resources needed to achieve it. To have such a life, a wide range of human rights are spelled out, among which are included the freedoms of speech, association and assembly; the right to health care and education; and the right to equal pay for equal work. The right to form and join a trade union is the only right found in all three documents. Governments are obligated to foster and promote these rights within a framework of the rule of law. Citizens must in turn have "duties to the community in which alone the free and full development" of the human personality is said to be possible. All bodies within society, including implicitly corporations, are obligated to act consistent with the principles of the Universal Declaration. As a unifying foundation for both domestic and foreign policy, there is no better guide for Canadian social democracy in the twenty-first century.

When I went to South Africa a few years ago, it was no surprise for me to find that Nelson Mandela saw in these rights and obligations the foundation for his country's new constitution. Nor with its narrow definition of democracy restricted to only political and civil rights and free market capitalism, is it surprising that the United States has not ratified the Covenant on Economic, Social and Cultural Rights.

POLITICS MATTERS

There is an important difference between the rights covenants when it comes to obligations for governments. Once ratified, a national government is obligated to implement without qualification the provisions of the Covenant on Civil and Political Rights. In general, this is what we did in Canada in 1982 with our Charter of Rights and Freedoms. On the other hand the Covenant on Economic, Social and Cultural Rights takes into account the different level of economic development among nations. This means that on-going political debate about priorities within any given country plays a crucial role. Ideology counts. Political leadership and political power matter. Decisions to spend or not to spend on a social right must be made. Will it be tax cuts or health care? Choosing of priorities *within* the family of social rights must also be done. How much for health care and how much for education?

Successful, functioning social democracies are the product of a positive and complex mix of ideology, political leadership, and institutional practice. Should a social democratic state modify or eliminate a significant number of universal social programs it would, of course, at some point cease to be social democratic. Just as the United States today can be seen as a liberal society that never aspired to social democratic status, so too could the Scandinavian and other European countries revert to a pre-social democratic character. We Canadians, who first came to describe ourselves as "sharing and caring" people only after years of strong universal social programs (health, pensions, unemployment insurance), could soon lose both the practice and the self-description. Recent policies of the federal and most provincial governments have undermined strong universal programs in health and education. The more these foundational institutions are changed, the less we will see ourselves as sharing and caring. We do not allocate political and civil rights on the basis of a means test. Nor should we do so with the right to health, post-secondary education or child care.

In seeking redress for the violation of either a political or a civil right, we naturally turn to the courts. In the case of social rights, redress requires a political act. Apart from the failure to implement a regulation, which may permit judicial review, disputes about the level of benefit of a social right, like its establishment in the first place are political issues. Values, leaders, and ideology count. Citizens acting as equals in the political process first established social rights. As we Canadians have seen, they can also be taken away in the same process.

INDIVIDUALISM: DIFFERENT VISIONS, DIFFERENT REALITIES

A social democracy should be seen for what it is: a principled, functioning, real alternative to the American-style liberal democracy favoured by Canada's flag-waving Liberals who prefer tax cuts to rebuilding and extending our social rights. The liberal sees an individual's life as unfolding in a society that stands in an antagonistic relationship to the state and in which citizens are essentially in competition with one another. The liberal then designs all institutions to make sure that they mesh with such a divisive goal.

We social democrats make different assumptions, beginning with the rejection of the competitive individualist model. Our rejection is *not* based on a utopian counter-vision, which naively sees humans as unalienated, altruistic beings. Instead it rests on a view of humanity that is much closer to reality than the caricature promoted by liberal individualism. Social democratic individualism incorporates cooperation. It is an individualism derived from an understanding of reality: human beings are inescapably social creatures and they have both personal and shared goals.

For the social democrat, there are two important universally observable qualities of human beings that should receive equal weight in assessments of potential economic and political structures – our disposition to pursue personal gain and our disposition to act cooperatively in implementing shared objectives with others. Most of us want personal and family satisfaction but we have also created in Canada 175,000 volunteer organizations to do things with and for our neighbours. We want to do such things within civil society *and* by means of government programs. Any polity that does not take into account these two basic human characteristics at best does a disservice to its citizens. Any proposed political agenda that puts its emphasis exclusively on either of these dispositions is seriously flawed.

The social democrat sees in his or her version of society, which matches a market driven economy with a regime of social rights, the answer to this century's most famous political question: what is to be done? Unlike the liberal, classical or neo, the social democrat sees the human capacity to cooperate as a practical and moral foundation for a global agenda for social rights and a healthy environment, objectives radically dissociated from market criteria. Unlike Marxists, old or new, the social democrat does acknowledge as productively useful our permanent disposition to seek our own benefit. A form of market-economy matched with social rights is not, therefore, either a compromise of liberal-democratic principles or some half-way step to a Marxist utopia. It is instead the best kind of society that can be constructed, given these two differing aspects of our nature. It provides for a broad range of individual and collective rights and for the opportunity for personal and community good. However, since the social democrat's deep commitment to political democracy entails the acceptance of pluralism, there will always be the option to broaden or narrow the degree of equality within society: to eliminate or maintain poverty, to recognize or withhold collective cultural identity rights for minorities, to respect or not divergence in sexual orientation, or to make bureaucracies more or less responsive to citizens.

Within the complex matrix of the democratic state, social democrats will normally be located among those supporting the first option in these pairs of choices at any given time – all of which expand human liberty for more people beyond the parameters set either by market forces or by tradition. However, competing political priorities can result in different decisions. Bad or mistaken leadership can also do so – as can the presence or absence of a vigorous civil society and the winning or losing of elections. Social democracy is a democracy and that means there can be no pre-determined outcomes. There is no golden calculator available as a guide to perfect solutions. Nor should there be in a free society.

CIVIL SOCIETY AND THE PARTY
The movement towards greater levels of equality has always

been a product of the interrelation between civil society and elected members of parliament. Many social democratic parties themselves emerged from the activism of unions and a variety of other groups within civil society, who had the goal of achieving political power in order to make changes in governmental policies. In Europe, through coalitions and majority governments, there has been remarkable political success at the national level in translating good policies into legislation that has benefited millions. Here in Canada, with New Democratic Party (NDP) governments at the provincial level and an effective presence of the NDP in Ottawa, rights and benefits for workers, pensioners, the sick, women, Aboriginal Peoples, visible minorities and gays and lesbians are much higher than in the United States, which lacks a social democratic party. Like any human institution, our party has experienced failures, set-backs and bad decisions. But any serious assessment based on egalitarian concerns would reach the same conclusion as Pierre Trudeau when he acknowledged that our presence has been a key element in bringing about progressive change in Canada. At the federal level in the 1980s and in the minority government a decade earlier, the NDP was significant in its impact. Canada has strong provisions in the Constitution Act of 1982 ensuring the equality rights of women and the historic rights of Aboriginal Peoples because of work done in civil society by the women's movement and Aboriginal leadership – and because the NDP was in Parliament, writing, persuading and moving adoption of key clauses.

The relationship between the Party and active groups within civil society is important and complex. When out of power, the Party is part of civil society, i.e. it is not a part of the governing structure and joins with other bodies in helping to shape public debate. However, unlike any other institution within civil society, it actually aspires to govern. It periodically goes to the people and asserts, if elected as a government, it would put in place such-and-such policies and laws, or if elected in opposition it would apply pressure to the elected government to adopt the same laws and policies.

In developing its political agenda the Party must listen to civil society. It must in particular take into account and learn from those groups who are closest to its philosophical orientation. But as a rule, it should neither seek nor accept affiliation with them. (The one exception is the trade union movement – to which I will return shortly). Women's groups, environmentalists, anti-poverty activists, and human rights organizations, student bodies, and the diverse groups critical of many aspects of corporate power and globalization: all of these provide needed critiques of the status quo and many provide thoughtful answers.

These advocacy groups are of great importance to democratic life. They bring serious matters to public attention and are often the major source of ideas for significant innovation by governments. To remain credible as organizations, they should remain completely independent of all political parties, promoting with integrity the particular agendas for what they believe needs to be done. They should attempt to influence all democratic parties although it is clear that some will be more open to their proposals than others. A social democratic party, for its part, must remain independent of them. This is not simply because within every category, e.g. environment, anti-poverty, human rights, there are groups whose agendas differ from one another, as well as groups that are knowledgeable and some that are not. More fundamentally, it is the Party's unique responsibility to translate a political critique into governmental action. In this sense, a political party is like no other group in civil society.

The Party must consider the evidence presented by a civil society organization. It must also take into account counter priorities and claims made by other groups and citizens. It must recommend so much spending for housing, education, and health – and do so in an accountable, responsible way to the community. An organization campaigning to eliminate child poverty can in good faith recommend the spending of so many millions of dollars to achieve this goal. A social democratic party cannot adopt the same agenda without first critically considering the amount of money needed to act on other social priorities. Only the Party as a civil society organization, whether in government or in opposition, has such serious and broad-ranging responsibility. If it promised without thinking and cannot deliver when elected, it shatters its own credibility. It must be prepared to say "no" before elections to many demands made by conscientious citizens because of its obligations to give equal consideration to the proposals of other conscientious citizens.

The trade union movement is the notable exception to the

general rule that civil society groups and the party should remain structurally independent and unaffiliated. There are a number of reasons for this. Many social democratic parties came into being because either wholly or in part they were created by trade unions. The NDP's birth in 1961 was the product of the Cooperative Commonwealth Federation (CCF), organized labour and individual progressive Canadians. Deeper than the mere fact of creation is the reason for it. In virtually all developed democracies, the trade union movement has as its *raison d'etre* the task of re-distributing power and income, for the benefit of workers. This is within the workplace the equivalent of the broader struggle for equality in society as a whole which is the hallmark of a social democratic party. It's no accident that in many communities across Canada, many of the executives of the first branches of the CCF and of the first trade union locals consisted of the same individuals. Organized labour, with leaders elected by its members, sees as its mission a struggle for justice for all men and women as workers (whether or not they are members of unions) and has seen in the party its preferred instrument for political change in society. This has provided a natural and unique fit between the Party and trade unions. No other group within civil society is in a similar position.

These strong ideological and institutional goals provide solid grounds for affiliation of trade union bodies within the party. (The question of providing funds for the party is an important but separate matter. See point (6) in my suggestions for a new political agenda at the end of this essay.) The Party and the trade union movement in Canada have been in strong agreement on most of the issues of the day – each providing input and support to the other. As autonomous organizations, however, they have differed, and on occasions these differences have been serious. This is inevitable and should not take away from the profound common agenda that they uniquely share: the building of a more egalitarian workplace and society.

THE FUTURE

As I indicated at the outset of this essay, in continental Europe where social democracy is most deeply imbedded in the minds and institutions of its citizens, the egalitarian essence of social citizenship continues to underpin the legislative agenda. In Canada, Britain and the United States, we have been moving backwards. Instead of encouraging market growth *within* a political framework of social justice, market and corporate priorities have been encouraged to dominate. Instead of countering the effects of market-produced inequality, the governments of Chrétien, Blair and Clinton have fostered it. The rich in all three countries have an increasing share of the after-tax income. (President Bush, with the support of Democrats, has exacerbated the problem with his recent tax measures.) Chrétien's recent election victory moved Canada even closer to a "low-tax" nation – i.e. one with poor social services like Britain and the United States. As a percentage of GDP, Blair's government is spending at about the same low level on social services as was Margaret Thatcher in 1984. It is actually allocating less to education.[3] In all three countries, the level of poverty, in general, and for children in particular, is impossible to find in any continental social democracy. We also find these Anglo-American governments' records on the environment lamentable. Once again, it was the Europeans who pushed for global reform at the Bonn meeting on the Kyoto environmental agreement in the summer of 2001.

The world recently celebrated the fiftieth anniversary of the Universal Declaration of Human Rights. That remarkable post-war document includes the much older political and civil rights as well as the new social and economic rights. Despite their birth dating back three hundred years, political and civil rights are still under attack, as seen in the continuing persecution and discrimination related to religious, ethnic, racial and sexual-orientation differences. Though vigilance on these rights is obviously essential, it is more than fortunate that the principle of political and civil rights has become deeply embedded in Canada and most other developed democracies. Citizens' rights involving the freedoms of religion, speech, assembly, association, voting and due process are defended quite vigorously by the establishment media as well as by academics and an active human rights community. However, this has not been the case with threats, abuses, or even clear violations of the social and economic rights which have been the major addition to the human rights agenda in this century. These rights require direct government intervention in the economy to alter its distributive effects on the side of equality. Editorial writers and virtually all political parties in Canada except the NDP are now the leading enemies of social and economic rights, in most cases ignorant of the fact that Canada committed itself to the Covenant on Economic, Social and Cultural Rights in 1976. While they readily denounce the emergence of ethnic cleansing or censorship, they either endorse or openly foster the dismantling of Canada's social rights. They appropriately insist that the democratic state, through our courts and parliaments must protect the right of an author to publish or a child with AIDS to go to a public school. But they readily acquiesce or even celebrate when a government dismantles a pension scheme, eliminates a housing benefit, or ignores the claim of workers to a union at home or abroad – all of which are internationally recognized human rights and favour those with less power and income. These rights are as central to human dignity as political and civil rights. While neo-liberals may revert to pre-Second World War standards of citizenship and remain ideologically consistent, social democrats cannot. Social democrats stand for more equality, or they stand for nothing.

We must not allow the avaricious aspects of current capitalism at home and abroad to wipe out the great postwar social reforms of this century. Policies that promote the removal of all "shackles" to the global movement of capital, now as in the nineteenth century, reveal the self-serving ideology of the dominant classes. Trade policies that protect the mobility and property rights of corporations but ignore the human rights of millions of workers are not neutral. They tip the balance in favour of the few over the many and foster the growing global inequality. The elites that advocate such policies need reminding that earlier in this century laissez-faire capitalism denied real freedoms to millions, exacerbated class conflict, and helped destroy some democracies while seriously destabilizing them all. Those young and old who today are demanding an end to unaccountable corporate power are involved in a struggle crucial to the future of democracy.

In addition to the fundamental need to keep and extend our social rights as citizens, other serious concerns about an unregulated market have also emerged in our time. If we are to preserve the environment on a sustainable basis, complete the struggle for gender equality, take into account the legitimate claims to identity of certain minorities, and foster the development of non-commercial cultural options, we require an activist government.

Only the mendacious or those ignorant of recent history can continue to argue that the Anglo-American neo-liberal version of capitalism on a global scale could possibly avoid either the serious social instability or the commercialized inequality that were its legacy for the nation state in the first half of the twentieth century.

The answers to the problems produced by economic globalization, whether in the North or South, are not to be found in either the economic status quo, or the rejection of markets as a key element in economic development. Rather, as two distinguished individuals have recently argued, the answer is to be found in combining markets with more and deeper democracy. Harvard economist Dani Rodrik has said national governments should be able to de-link from international trade obligations when they conflict with deeply held national norms and values. Amartya Sen, the Nobel prize winner in Economics, has made a similar but broader-ranging democratic argument. In effect, the kind of social democratic development that has already produced economic growth in the context of equality and freedom within a handful of the world's democracies must be deepened at home and extended on a global basis.

We must reject outright the economic neo-liberal and institutional conservatism of the Liberal government in Ottawa. To achieve true citizen's equality in Canada we need significant improvements in fleshing out both our political and social rights. Parliamentary and electoral reform is badly needed. Our cities need new powers. To help build a better world, we must be efficient and support trade but insist that globalization include rules that will ensure that when in conflict, the human rights and environmental needs of democratic peoples will trump the trading-based property rights of corporations. In Parliament in 1982 we rejected proposals to include property rights in the Constitution. We did so because of the fear that such entrenchment would lead to legal disputes which could jeopardize the more fundamental social and environmental priorities decided upon by elected legislators. What we sensibly decided in 1982 should be rejected in domestic law is now embodied in international trade agreements. This is absurd and anti-democratic – and must be changed.

During the coming years, the only way the important domestic and international proposals for reform made by social democrats, human rights, environment, poverty, and women's groups earlier this year at Quebec City will be implemented is by change in domestic and international law. This will happen in Canada neither by remaining in the streets nor as a consequence of good arguments. Protest and reason are never sufficient in a democracy. Change has occurred in Canada at the national level when the Liberals saw demonstrations and arguments directly reinforced by the possibility of electoral defeat in Parliament. This has happened when federal governments were confronted by a principled party on the left which is committed to winning elections. In 1945, Mackenzie King took significant steps towards the creation of the Canadian welfare state. It was not a coincidence that he did so only after the Cooperative Commonwealth Federation had almost won Ontario in 1943, formed a government in Saskatchewan in 1944, and led national public opinion polls for the first time in 1945. Medicare became a national reality only after the NDP won power and showed it could be done at the provincial level. Political power matters, but so does the threat of losing it.

Canada's social democratic party, the NDP, is now going through a serious and positive process of renewal. Its members can be proud of its contributions to Canada. It now needs a revised structure, an updated agenda, and a new name. The Party should be finally called "social democrat" because that is what it has been for forty years. What will not change is its profound commitment to equality which is what makes it unique in our history.

As mentioned earlier, the Universal Declaration of Human Rights embodies the fundamental values of social democracy. This political and economic philosophy is spelled out in greater detail in the International Bill of Rights which includes the Universal Declaration on Human Rights, as well as the Covenant on Economic, Social and Cultural Rights, and the Covenant on Civil and Political Rights. By 1976, Canada had committed itself to all three. These obligations to extend liberty and broaden equality by enlarging the scope of civil, economic, political and social rights provide benchmarks against which we can measure human progress at home and abroad. For Canadians, they could serve as a major source of inspiration. For the Party, they should serve as guideposts for charting the direction of future national and international policies. What follows are some suggestions for future development in these areas:

1) A critique of the federal Liberals' failure to live up to their domestic and international obligations contained in the Covenant on Economic, Social and Cultural Rights, complemented by related concrete policy proposals, particularly on low-income housing and child poverty.

2) Detailed policy suggestions aimed at overcoming the lack of democratic transparency and accountability in international trade discussions and institutions, particularly those associated with the WTO, regional trade agreements, and global financial institutions. As one component of needed reforms, Canada should be insisting that when there is a conflict between an international human right and any provision in a trade agreement, the right should trump. This is what our Charter of Rights and Freedoms means at home. The same principle should hold internationally.

3) Proposals aimed at bringing civil society organizations and government officials into forums of regular engagement on policy matters. These forums would have to respect the ultimate independence of each but would encourage ongoing exchange on contemporary concerns.

4) A comprehensive and specific strategy to translate the Kyoto agreement on climate change into action. A Party policy committee could be mandated to show specifically how we can have sustainable development *and* concentrate on new industries that can take advantage of a growing global demand for equipment and machinery related to sources of energy other than petroleum.

5) A carefully thought out agenda for making corporations more accountable to their employees and their national and international communities, as well as their shareholders. Trade unions have already made significant progress in redistributing the benefits of a market economy by negotiating higher wages, improved health and safety standards,

better pensions, and extended vacations for their members, thereby raising standards for working men and women generally. But much more is required, notably in the international context involving human rights (which include workers' rights) and the environment. Specific reform ideas for domestic and international institutional change are available. They need to be translated into concrete policies to be brought before the people of Canada and the international community.

6) Finally, major reforms to broaden the political rights of citizenship. For example:

    a) The Party should lead the way in proposing and promoting a thought–out, revised, democratic electoral system, one which would combine elements of the existing single member constituency with proportional representation.

    b) Corporations and unions and all other collective entities should be banned from financially contributing to federal political parties and candidates. The governments of Quebec and Manitoba made such democratic reform by insisting that apart from the government itself, only individual Canadians should be allowed to provide money for either parties or individuals seeking political office. This moves to much more equality in a citizen's capacity to influence policy debates and electoral results.

---

[1] An earlier version of some of the arguments made here first appeared in "Social Democracy or Liberalism in the New Millennium" in Peter Russell (ed.) *The Future of Social Democracy.* Toronto: University of Toronto Press, 1999.

[2] In reading a document released on July 26, 2001, by a group who want either a significantly changed New Democratic Party or a new party, a person from Mars could be excused for thinking that the second half of the twentieth century had somehow disappeared. This statement, "The

New Politics Initiative: open, sustainable, democratic," contains four references to social democracy, all of which are pejorative. The movement and its leaders are portrayed as "condescending", acting "from on high", or a "paternalistic elite". Its accomplishments in Canada and elsewhere in the world are ignored. The positive legacy of thousands of party activists and leaders alike in Canada and throughout the world are simply passed over. It's a virtual certainty that none of the drafters of this document would describe themselves as supporters of a social democratic philosophy. The level of discussion about markets is best indicated by MP Svend Robinson, a member of the coordinating committee of the New Politics Initiative. At a conference at McGill University in May, 2001, Mr. Robinson did not agree with the serious arguments being made by social democratic economists that markets should be tamed or made subservient to broader social goals, including equality. "Markets," he said, "like mad dogs, should be put down."

[3] *See* Tony Judt, "'Twas a Famous Victory," *New York Review of Books*. July 19, 2001.

Why Can't Canada Be More Like Denmark?

ANDREW JACKSON

IT HAS BEEN ARGUED FROM BOTH SIDES OF THE POLITI-
cal spectrum that neo-liberal globalization sets in train irresistible
pressures to the 'downward harmonization' of social standards, and
forces countries to conform to the minimalist social welfare/high
inequality US model. Downward pressures driven by international
competition do exist, particularly with respect to progressive taxes
and redistributive income transfers. (Key provisions in international
trade and investment agreements also constrain progressive social
policy). However, progressive social policy sustains not just social
justice but also good economic performance. If there is anything to
the argument that so-called human capital and social capital are a
fundamentally important part of any economy, and a still more
important part of a knowledge based economy, then progressive
social policy should promote economic efficiency as well as social
equity. (Jackson, 2000a; Osberg, 1995).

This seems to be the case since there is surprisingly little evidence of downward harmonization of social policy or a generalized

shift to greater after tax income inequality across the advanced industrial (OECD) countries. While inequality has increased in the US and Canada, some European countries, notably Denmark and the Netherlands, have been able to maintain high levels of social welfare and relatively equal societies while also participating successfully in the 'new global economy.'

DOWNWARD HARMONIZATION?

The evidence for OECD countries clearly shows that there was no correlation between low taxes and high economic growth, and no correlation between high income inequality and high economic growth in the 1980s and 1990s. (Jackson 2000 a,b; Arjona, 2001). The US turned in a good growth performance in the second half of the 1990s and achieved very low unemployment, but so did some countries with high taxes, strong labour movements and generous welfare states, notably Denmark and the Netherlands (Auer, 2000). If the US grew faster in the 1990s than much of continental Europe and Canada, it was because of low interest rates and not regressive social policies. Unlike European Central banks, Alan Greenspan allowed the expansion to continue even as unemployment fell below levels which had once been feared as too inflationary. New technology helped a lot, but productivity growth in Europe has generally at least matched US levels.

Despite all the fears of downward harmonization to a minimalist welfare state, OECD data clearly show that public social spending has increased rather than fallen as a share of GDP, with the OECD average rising from 19.3% in 1980 to 22.1% in 1990, to 23.5% in 1997, (Arjona, 2001). In almost all countries, social spending has increased at least in line with GDP growth, though Canada in recent years has been a major exception. Moreover, it is not true to say that there has been a generalized shift to greater income inequality in OECD countries in the 1980s and 1990s.

There has indeed been a trend towards greater market income inequality arising from the impacts of high unemployment and more precarious jobs on low income households, and from the growing market income share of the most affluent. Income inequality caused by differences in levels of employment and unemployment varies a great deal between countries, but there has been a significant overall tendency for the market income share of the most affluent part of the working age population to rise somewhat at the expense of the middle and the bottom. This rising market income share of the elite can be linked to globalisation to some degree. However, when it comes to the distribution of income after taxes and transfers, there has been no general shift towards greater inequality, suggesting that many countries have actually redistributed market income more actively in the 1980s and 1990s than in the heyday of the welfare state (Forster, 2000). If there is a trend, it is towards increased income inequality in those countries that were most unequal to begin with because of deregulated labour markets and a low level of social spending. After tax/transfer income inequality has grown from already extreme levels in the US, has risen sharply in the UK, and has begun to rise in Canada since the mid 1990s. But there has been little or no increase in after tax income inequality in already relatively high equality countries such as Denmark, the Netherlands and Germany (Jackson, 2000a).

GLOBALIZATION AND THE PERSISTENCE OF DIFFERENCES IN SOCIAL WELFARE

Quite different forms of capitalism continue to exist despite all of the talk of globalization driven convergence to a minimalist welfare model. Table 1, provides some key economic and social indicators for Canada, the US, and Denmark. The latter has the highest tax burden in the OECD, and currently spends almost 50 cents directly on the public sector – that is, on health, education, housing, recreation, child and elder care, community services and so on (everything excluding transfers)– for every dollar of private spending, double the level in the US. Public social spending is 30% of GDP, almost double the US and Canadian level. More than 2 in 3 workers are covered by collective agreements, almost double the Canadian level, which is in turn almost double the US level. Denmark is a startlingly more egalitarian society than the US or Canada. The starting point of the top 10% of earners is only a bit more than twice as much as the cut-off for the bottom 10%, compared to more than 4 times as much in the US, and slightly less in Canada. Less than 1 in 10 working women are low paid (earning less than two-thirds the median wage) compared to more than 1 in 3 in Canada and the US. The after tax incomes of the top 10% start at only about 3 times more than the cut-off for the bottom 10% compared to more than 6

LATE 1990S STATISTICS COMPARED

	US	Canada	Denmark	Note
GDP per capita at PPP	100	81	87	1998
Growth of GDP per Capita	1.70%	1.00%	2.30%	Annual, 1990-98
Men, 45 hrs.+	26%	22%	15%	Long Working Time
Taxes as % GDP	28.50%	36.80%	52.20%	1998
Ratio Public/ Private Spending	0.24	0.36	0.48	Transfers Not Included
Public Social Spending	16%	17%	30%	% GDP
Collective Bargaining	18%	36%	69%	% Workers Covered
Male Earnings D10/D1	4.3	3.8	2.2	Bottom of D10/ Top D1
Low Paid Women	32.50%	34.30%	8.00%	<2/3 median wage
Income D10/D1	6.44	3.93	2.86	After tax; bottom of D10/top of D1
Child Poverty	22.70%	13.90%	4.00%	<1/2 medain

Sources: See Jackson 2000a

times higher in the US, and about 4 times higher in Canada. Child poverty is negligible.

While Denmark has a dollar standard of living which is 87% of the US level, if GDP per person were to be adjusted for shorter hours worked by the full-time employed and for an equitable distribution of income, then Denmark would win hands down. After all, the modest income advantage of being an American only goes to the top layer who appropriate a disproportionate share of total national income.

This key fact is often glossed over in Canada, leaving many Canadians with the impression that middle-class Americans are better off. In fact, even with per capita GDP in Canada adjusted for living costs now being about 20% lower than in the US and income taxes being somewhat higher, Statistics Canada has calculated that the bottom 25% of Canadian households have after tax incomes which are much higher than the bottom 25% in the US, and that the median US household is only 7% better off than the median Canadian household. Moreover, that US household will have to spend 11% of after tax income on health care, compared to 4.6% in Canada, wiping out the dollar advantage. (Wolfson and Murphy, 2000.) Only the top 20% or so of Canadians would gain by moving to the low tax/low social spending US, assuming that they wanted to be top dogs in a dog eat dog society.

Turning back to Denmark, there was no increase in after tax/transfer inequality in the 1990s, no decline in unionization, expansion rather than shrinkage of the public sector, and reform rather than retrenchment of the welfare state. Far from becoming an economic basket case, doomed to failure and stagnation by its quaint and outmoded attachment to out of date egalitarian goals, Denmark turned in an economic growth performance at least as good as the US in the 1990s, and currently has an unemployment rate of less than 5%, just as low as the US. More than 75% of the working age population have jobs, even higher than in the US. It may not be easy, but it is certainly possible to reconcile a high level of social welfare with growth and job creation in the new world order. (Madsen, 1999)

Social Democratically led Denmark has also led the way in Europe in terms of promoting environmental sustainability, and there has been a lively national debate between social democrats and a strong left/green party . The labour movement is strong and active. Notwithstanding close links to the government – Prime Minister Rasmussen is the former chief economist of the main union confederation – unions recently led a successful national strike for a sixth week of paid holidays.

It has to be conceded that while some other relatively equal countries such as the Netherlands did well in the 1990s, others, such as Sweden, did not fare so well. The evidence shows that there is no link from high taxes and high social spending to lower growth, not that equality and progressive social policy lead to stronger growth. Further, there were some modest signs of downward harmonization in Denmark and other social democratic countries in the 1990s. Corporate tax rates have been lowered, along with the highest personal tax rates. The overall tax burden in OECD countries has not been harmonized down, but the mix of taxes has shifted to more regressive taxes, such as payroll and sales taxes to some degree as corporations and the affluent have indeed used the threat of packing their bags to demand cuts for themselves. However, from the standpoint of achieving equality, a highly progressive tax system is less important than having an equitable distribution of wage income, and a high level of spending on income transfers and on public services. Even Swedish social democracy in its heyday depended very little on steeply progressive taxes to achieve income equality.

Also not to be simplistic, it has to be conceded that in Denmark, as in the Netherlands and other successful smaller European countries, there were some significant reforms to social security in the 1990s. (Auer, 2000.) So-called 'passive' transfers to the unemployed were reduced – though not very significantly – and the focus was placed very much on strategies to integrate the working age unemployed and marginalised into the job market. Some have seen this as an accommodation of social welfare objectives to the need for global competitiveness. But the rejigging of social security to meet labour market needs took place in a very different context from similar so-called reforms in Canada, the US and Britain. Denmark as well as the Netherlands achieved strong gains in employment in labour markets where wages are still relatively equal and where low pay is rare. While social security reform in the US and Canada has pushed many from welfare into very low wage work, reform in parts of Europe has provided real ladders of opportunity.

While the US and Canada used the stick of welfare and E.I. cuts, Denmark and the Netherlands have maintained generous unemployment benefits while also investing heavily in training. Denmark and Sweden spend more than 6% of GDP on active labour market policies, compared to 1.2% in Canada and just 0.8% in the US. (Arjona, 2001.)

NEGATIVE PRESSURES FROM GLOBALIZATION ON PROGRESSIVE SOCIAL POLICY

The three key mechanisms of progressive social policy which promote greater equality of conditions and life chances in capitalist societies are: labour market policies to promote high employment and a reasonably equal distribution of wage income; tax and transfer policies to redistribute market income; and the establishment of a large non market sector to provide some services on the basis of citizenship rather than ability to pay. Advocates of neo-liberal globalization tend to believe that each of these mechanisms inhibit economic efficiency and competitiveness, and will thus have to be substantially modified in the new global order, while many critics of globalization who support these equality producing social policies believe that they are subject to erosion in a world of mobile capital.

Collective bargaining and high minimum labour standards unambiguously produce greater wage equality but are seen by most corporations as a source of costly 'rigidities' North American corporations seemingly prefer, all things being equal, to produce and invest in low labour standard US states and in Mexico, resulting in downward pressures on more progressive Canadian policies. However, studies do show that unionization and high labour standards tend to go hand in hand with higher productivity and can facilitate workplace change. (Auer, 2000; Jackson , 2000a.) Canada's unionization rate has not declined significantly under the FTA and NAFTA, though labour rights and standards have probably been harmonized down to some degree.

The tendency of globalization to harmonize down corporate and top income tax rates has been noted, and there are probably downward pressures on income transfers to at least the working age population. E.I. and social assistance cuts in Canada in the 1990s were driven to some degree by fiscal, cost-cutting considerations, but also by the view that 'generous' social provision discourages acceptance of low wage work, thus artificially increasing wages and undermining competitiveness. The Department of Finance and the OECD have both argued that E.I. and social assistance cuts were needed to help secure labour market flexibility and low inflation. Low inflation as well as balanced budgets are certainly at a premium in a world of hyper mobile financial capital.(Jackson 2000c.) It can be noted that the countries which have maintained progressive social policies have tended to insulate themselves against financial market pressures by being impeccably orthodox when it has come to balancing budgets and keeping inflation low and stable. Certainly Denmark benefited from balancing its budget early, and even had room to provide some fiscal stimulus to job growth in the early 1990s downturn.

While increased international competition likely sets in train pressures to cut redistributive income transfers, it is less clear why the decision to maintain a large non market social sector would be directly affected. Canada and the US and indeed all advanced industrial countries spend approximately the same share of GDP on social protection, broadly defined. (Arjona, 2001; Larsson, 1998.) The major difference is in the public/private split of these costs. The US spends 7.1% of GDP on private health care compared to 2.7% in Canada, and health care consumes 11.2% of US after tax family budgets compared to 4.6% in Canada. A greater focus on the market does not reduce total social protection costs, but rather shifts them onto households, while greatly increasing inequality of access to services.(For example, 8 out of 10 low income Canadians (bottom quintile) visit a doctor annually, compared to 6 in 10 in the US.) (Wolfson, 2000.) There is strong evidence that public provision of health care is more efficient in narrow cost terms than private delivery, and the same is true of other services and programs, from education to pensions. While parts of the corporate sector would benefit directly from a shift from public to private delivery, it is far from clear that this would promote increased international competitiveness of the corporate sector as a whole.

There are, indeed, some plausible links from globalization in the sense of intensified international competition for production and investment to 'downward harmonization' of some equality producing social policies. At least some high equality countries were not economically marginalised in the 1990s, have not harmonized down, and have not become more unequal. This suggests that there are offsetting positive linkages from progressive social policies to good economic performance.

POSITIVE LINKS FROM PROGRESSIVE SOCIAL POLICY TO ECONOMIC PERFORMANCE

One key linkage from equality to so-called human capital is in the area of health. Research has shown that, beyond a certain level of national income, the positive link between rising average income and health disappears, such that the modest differences in average income between advanced industrial countries have no impact on population health. At the same time, there is a gradient of health status based on income in all countries, with higher income groups enjoying better health and longer lives, and lower income groups dying relatively earlier and enjoying fewer years of disability free health. The gradient which links health status to income varies significantly between different countries, and is much flatter where income is most equally distributed. In short, what matters for health in advanced industrial countries is not the absolute level of income at any point of the income distribution, but how equally income is distributed. This can be explained by the negative psychological and social impacts of inequality on the less well-off, and by the greater exposure of lower income groups to health risks at work, in the home and in the community. Further, high equality societies almost always have a high level of public involvement in health care, which is largely delivered outside of the market mechanism and thus serves all income groups more or less equally. (Ross, 2000.)

Consider the example of Canada and the United States. It is common to note that Medicare is a competitive advantage for Canada in the sense that companies do not have to pay as large a share of employee health care costs. But it is less common to note that higher income equality in Canada combined with a much less marketised and commodified health care system have resulted in significantly higher levels of population health. The most recent data from the World Health Organization show that Canadians can, on average, expect to live for 79 years, 72 years of which will be lived free of disability and in good health. In the US, both average life expectancy and disability adjusted life expectancy at birth are 2 years less than in Canada, and the US ranks 24th in the world by the latter measure, while Canada ranks 12th.

Research by Michael Wolfson of Statistics Canada and others has linked mortality to income inequality at the state and provincial level and at the level of large urban areas. (Ross, 2000.) There is a clear link between the two, with annual mortality among working age adults falling from 675 per 100,000 in the most unequal US states, to 400 or less per 100,000 in the most equal US states and in the Canadian provinces, all of which are at the high equality end of the North American spectrum. Based on the calculated link from income inequality to mortality, it can be said that if the US had the same income distribution as Canada, close to 100,000 fewer working age Americans would die each year. This in turn translates into markedly higher incidence in the US of a range of chronic conditions which lead to disability as well as premature death.

A second key dimension of so-called human capital is literacy and numeracy. Again, research shows that countries differ not just in terms of average literacy and numeracy levels, but also in terms of the distribution of literacy and numeracy skills within the population. As with health, there is much flatter gradient of literacy and numeracy levels in more egalitarian societies. Take the prose literacy level of young adults, as measured in a comparable way across countries in the International Adult Literacy Survey. As shown in the Chart, the mean literacy rate is higher in Sweden (representative of the Scandinavian countries) than in Canada, which is in turn slightly higher than the US. The gap in scores is very small for the top 25% in each of the three countries, with Sweden very slightly ahead, but the gap is much larger between the lower achievers. If we take the bottom 25% and particularly the bottom 5%, Sweden does far better, and Canada does much better than the US. Other research based on this survey has shown that the link from parental socio-economic status to literacy and numeracy achievement is much weaker in the high equality Scandinavian and Benelux countries than in Canada, which in turn equalizes achievement levels more than the US. Further, there is a strong and unsurprising linkage from literacy and numeracy levels to individual success in the labour market.

What can we conclude from these gradients of 'human capital' by income? First, there is overwhelming evidence that high in-

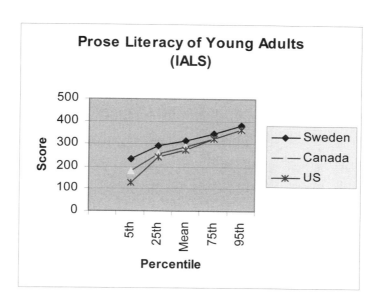

come equality translates into much broader equality of life chances. A child born into a low income family in Denmark has a better chance of lifetime good health and a better chance of acquiring the skills needed to obtain a good education and rewarding employment than a comparable child in Canada, and a Canadian child has a better chance than one born in the US. While the differences are most significant for those at the bottom, they are probably not insignificant for middle-class children. These differences are plausibly linked to both more equal income distribution, which tends to equalize conditions, opportunities and life chances by equalizing market consumption, and to a high level of quality public services. Health care for low income Canadians is superior to that in the US and, in the case of literacy and numeracy, we can reasonably believe that schools in low income neighbourhoods in Canada are of better quality than schools in low income neighbourhoods in the US.

For those of us concerned with social welfare and social justice, the case for greater income equality and for a larger public sector is confirmed. But what about economic efficiency and international competitiveness in the new global economy? It could, perhaps, be argued that what counts in the new global economy is the skills, talents and capacities of the top 20%, or of a still narrower elite, and that the health, skills and 'human capital' of the rest of society are of little account. But this is surely absurd, and economists of almost all persuasions are all but unanimous on the need to invest in the 'human capital' of the entire population to achieve success in the new, 'knowledge-based' global economy.

Further, high equality fosters a high level of social co-operation or 'social capital.'. Part of the Danish success story in the 1990s has been bargained reforms to social policy through negotiations involving unions, employers and the government – not unilateral imposition of change – and full employment oriented collective bargaining. Danish unions have raised real wages and maintained a high wage floor, but have also co-operated to maintain a low inflation and 'investment friendly' climate. While controversial on parts of the left, bargaining to achieve key macro economic and distributional outcomes was very much a feature of successful social democracy in the Golden Age of the 1960s (as in the solidarity wages policy in Sweden.) And there is no contradiction between a strong union role in the workplace and high productivity.

CONCLUSION

The central conclusion to be drawn from the recent experiences of some smaller European countries – notably Denmark and the Netherlands – is that relative economic success in today's globalized capitalism can still be achieved despite, or even because of, continuing relative equality of income and life chances.

Denmark has a very high level of collective bargaining coverage, a relatively egalitarian wage structure, and a highly equal distribution of national income. This is a profoundly different society than the U.S. or Canada and much more attractive for those of us who value the goals of equality and solidarity. Further, inequality and insecurity have not been increasing in the 1990s, despite some "reform" of tax systems and welfare state programs. Denmark has achieved strong rates of employment growth and low unemployment, and rates of per capita GDP growth and productivity growth that match or exceed those of the U.S. While highly export-oriented and highly integrated into regional (European) and even global markets, Denmark has succeeded in international competition in the 1990s through a renewed "social pact" which has maintained real wage growth and have been associated with the reduction of working time and the maintenance of generally good employment conditions. "Flexibility" has been negotiated, but decent standards have been preserved and inequality and low-wage work have been contained. At a minimum, a regulated labour market is no barrier to high productivity and high-quality production, and there is support for the argument that high productivity is promoted by collective bargaining and advanced welfare states.

It is worth considering what Canada might look like if we decided to emulate Denmark rather than the United States, and succeeded in doing so. Both government spending and taxes as a share of GDP would rise by almost 50%, allowing for an enormous expansion of income transfer programs and public services. Collective bargaining coverage would double, low-wage work would practically disappear, and the pay gap between the top and bottom of the earnings distribution would shrink from at least 4:1 to 2:1. Child poverty would be all but eliminated, and household income inequality would be hugely reduced. Furthermore, if the Danish experience is anything to go by, per capita GDP and productivity would be essentially unchanged and we would enjoy sustained growth of living standards. Making Canada look more like Denmark would constitute a rather radical social transformation.

It is true, of course, that Canada is not Denmark, and our close integration with the U.S. exposes us to harmonization pressures with respect to taxes, spending and labour market regulation that are more significant than those in the EU. Nor are we a small and cohesive society determined to maintain an advanced model of social solidarity. But it can certainly be suggested that the barriers to such a social democratic project are more political than structural.

There are no compelling reasons why Canadians could not put job creation at the forefront of economic and social policy, based on much higher levels of co-operation among business, labour and governments. There are no compelling reasons why growing fiscal surpluses could not be devoted in much greater measure to investments in social programs and income supports, given that these investments could be expected to have positive impacts on long-term productivity and not just on greater equality of outcomes. Canada is very different from the smaller European countries on many dimensions, but that does not negate what can be learned from them about positive co-operation at the workplace, training and labour adjustment policies, real investment in the long-term unemployed and income supports for low-skilled workers, and so on.

REFERENCES

Arjona, Roman, Maxime Ladaique and Mark Pearson. "Growth, Inequality and Social Protection." Draft OECD paper presented to the IRPP-CSLS Conference on Linkages Between Economic Growth and Inequality, Ottawa, Jan. 26-27th. 2001. (Available from www.csls.ca.)

Auer, Peter. *Employment Revival in Europe: Labour Market Success in Austria, Denmark, Ireland and the Netherlands.* International Labour Organisation. Geneva. 2000.

Forster, Michael. "Trends and Driving Factors in Income Distribution and Poverty in the OECD Area." OECD Labour Market and Social Policy Occasional Paper No. 42. OECD, 2000. (Available from www.oecd.org.)

Jackson, Andrew. "Can There Be a Second Way in the Third Millennium?" *Studies in Political Economy.* Summer, 2001.

Jackson, Andrew. *Why We Don't Have to Choose Between Social Justice and Economic Growth: The Myth of the Equity-Efficiency Trade-Off.* Canadian Council on Social Development, 2000. (Available from www.ccsd.ca.)

Jackson, Andrew. "Tax Cuts: The Implications for Growth and Productivity." *Canadian Tax Journal* Vol. 48 #2, 2000.

Larsson, Allan. "Social Protection and Economic Performance" in David Foden and Peter Morris (Eds.) *The Search for Equity: Welfare and Security in the Global Economy.* Lawrence and Wishart. London. 1998.

Madsen,, Per Kongshoj. "Denmark: Flexibility, Security and Labour Market Success." International Labour Organisation, Employment and Training Paper #53, 1999
OECD with Statistics Canada. *Literacy in the Information Age: Final Report of the International Adult Literacy Survey.* 2000.

Osberg, Lars. "The Equity-Efficiency Trade-off in Retrospect." *Canadian Business Economics.* Vol. 3#3. Spring, 1995.

Ross, Nancy, Michael C. Wolfson, James R. Dunn, Jean-Marie Berthelot and George A. Kaplan ; "Relation Between Income Inequality and Mortality in Canada and the United States: Cross Sectional Assessment Using Census Data and Vital Statistics." *British Medical Journal* Vol. 320. April 1, 2000.

Statistics Canada. "Health Status of Children". *Health Reports* Vol. 11 #3. Winter, 1999.

Wolfson, M. "On the Health of Canadians Across the 49th Parallel." Paper presented at Queen's University Institute for Social Policy, 2000.

Wolfson, M. and B. Murphy. "Income Inequality in North America: Does the 49th Parallel Still Matter?" Statistics Canada. Canadian Economic Observer. Cat. 11-010-XPB. August, 2000.

Dangerous Imports from Brazil?
Lessons in Participatory Democracy

DAVID LANGILLE

When the canadian government banned beef from Brazil, it should have been more worried about importing their radical politics which are so threatening to the neo-liberal model of corporate globalization. These exciting political experiments being undertaken by the PT, the Partido dos Trabalhadores, (Workers Party) offer an alternative, an example that demonstrates 'a different world is possible.'

That helps to explain why the first World Social Forum was held in Porto Alegre, Brazil, the city which now bills itself as the 'capital of democracy.' While the world's economic elite gathered in Davos, Switzerland, 14,000 activists met in the South to discuss alternative visions. What made the event such a success was the inspiration and organization provided by the democratic socialist governments of the city of Porto Alegre and the state of Rio Grande do Sul. The Brazilians showed that the best way to begin the fight against corporate globalization is to have strong social movements, to elect a progressive political party, and to strengthen the public sector via participatory democracy.[1]

The first impression for a Canadian arriving in Brazil is one of size -the realization that Brazil is the fifth largest country in the world, with the sixth largest population, nearing 170 million. Brazil not only dominates South America, it is the eighth largest economy in the world, with a GNP of US$ 778 billion.[2] Although they report an annual per capita income of $4,420, the distribution is so skewed that half the people there earn only the minimum wage of $77 a month or less than $924 per year.[3] Brazil's executives, on the other hand, are among the highest paid in the world. Their luxury condominiums stand in stark contrast to the hillside favellas and to the squatters shacks of cardboard and plastic.

Brazil is a country of gross inequality, of "social apartheid" according to the PT. The Brazilians pay a high price for this inequality in crime and corruption, in security guards and in personal insecurity. The point came forcefully home to me when I arrived to find a dead body outside my hotel in Rio de Janeiro. The corpse had been laying there for six hours after the man was shot by police. Such violence help explain why the middle class thinks Brazil needs more social justice, and why many are voting for the Workers Party.

The city of Porto Alegre demonstrates that politics can make a difference. There, the Workers Party has won four terms of office with increasing majorities. The United Nations points to the city as a model of good public administration, and even the World Bank celebrates its efficient economic management.[4] Porto Alegre appears clean, relatively safe and comparably affluent, like many cities in southern Europe. There are still substantial pockets of poverty, and prostitutes still work the streets, but the mood is of hope and possibilities.

What was most striking for a Northerner at the World Social Forum was to witness the passion, the energy and the excitement when the leaders of the Workers Party entered the auditorium. The thousands of Brazilians in the room went wild, with both young and old cheering, singing, waving and whistling. I wondered what these politicians, such as Lula da Silva, the national leader, and Olivio Dutra, the state governor, are doing to inspire such enthusiasm.

As the Canadian left struggles to find a new political vehicle, wrestling with whether to re-vitalize the NDP, to transform it or transcend it, we could look to the PT of Brazil for inspiration. Of course, the PT is a product of its own special circumstances, and much is not transferable. We cannot import the Brazilian model, or even pin our hopes on the PT'S success. But from the PT we should be open to recieve new ideas and successful innovations.

The experience of the PT addresses two of the great dilemmas that have afflicted the NDP over the past 30 years. The first is the disconnect between the party and Canada's social movements. As Walter Young recounts in his classic history of the CCF, the strength of the early CCF came from its strong base in the socio-economic movements of Saskatchewan - the cooperatives and credit unions, the farmers organizations and womens' groups, etc.[5] The PT shows how a party can maintain the support of very radical yet quite autonomous social movements. Another weakness of the NDP has been its relatively poor support from Canada's intellectual community, particularly from university faculty and students. This 'brain drain' stems in large part from the expulsion of the Waffle tendency which advocated for a stronger commitment to economic nationalism and socialism in the early Seventies. This disconnect has cost the party in terms of creative communications and policy depth, which is most notable when the party gains office and finds itself short of skilled economists and other policy experts. From the PT we might learn how to retain intellectual vibrancy and commitment.

As we will see, the Workers Party offers both substantive and procedural changes to the status quo - new policies and new politics. Its victories at the municipal and state level mean that it has been able to put into practice "its novel and imaginative ideas about direct democracy, which have made the party into the largest and most exciting laboratory of left-wing politics in the world."[6]

THE WORKERS PARTY

The PT was born in the struggle against the military dictatorship which began in 1964, a time of repression, censorship, political persecution, torture, murder and exile. The Brazilian Economic Miracle of the 1970's depended on a wage freeze and the control of trade union activity. Following a wave of strikes from 1978-80, it was evident that workers could not expect economic gains until they applied political pressure to end military rule. These protests were centred on the burgeoning industrial capital of Sao Paulo. Much of the leadership came from the Metalworkers Union, and its president, Lula da Silva, who was among those arrested and jailed for strike activity.

In 1980, militants such as Lula formed the Workers Party in order to express the political aspirations of a variety of social movements, including labour. The new party unified the struggles of students who had been marching for democratic freedoms, neighbourhood associations who were seeking paved streets, public transit and schools, and housewives who wanted daycare, medical care, and an end to poverty. Women, blacks and homosexuals found a new voice. The Brazilian churches were bastions of liberation theology, and the church's grassroots communities served as an important organizational base for the PT. The party not only attracted left-wing militants of various persuasions, it appealed to a variety of professionals - doctors, professors, lawyers, journalists and public servants. A final, critical ingredient was the growing movement of the landless, the Movimento dos Trabalhadores Rurais Sem Terra (Landless Rural Workers Movement, or MST), whose daring occupations of "unproductive" land captured the imagination of many Brazilians. The MST had an ambitious program of re-socializing the rural populace, re-settling the urban poor, reinventing community life, and fostering organic agriculture.[7]

Despite the widespread call for a rapid end to the dictatorship, the 1980's were marked by a gradual extension of political freedoms. Although the trappings of democracy were in place, there was widespread electoral fraud and continued violence in the countryside, with priests and union leaders being assassinated. When the military finally withdrew from public office, the Workers Party found their leading opponent was the Social Democratic Party, whose leader, Fernando Henrique Cardoso had ONCE been a well-known leftist professor. But in the 1990's under Cardoso's leadership, the party and the government became the champions of neo-liberalism and avid crusaders for market-oriented economic restructuring.

The economic elite has rallied behind Cardoso because he offers an alternative to the growing threat of the Workers Party. But the neo-liberal model of economic growth which he advocates is ill-equipped to resolve the glaring inequality. The deregulation and dismantling of the welfare state serves to widen the disparities. Although Cardoso managed to curb inflation for a few years, the economy is increasingly vulnerable to the vagaries of international finance. Attempts to raise the minimum wage and pensions for the elderly are resisted because of IMF pressure to cut public spending.

Wheras the neo-liberal model "weakens parties, demeans politics, further reduces the electoral process to marketing games and media manipulation, and demobilizes the population,"[8] the Workers Party offers an alternative that attracts growing support. The PT now has 750,000 "affiliates"and over 2000 "regional directorates", each of which contains many "nucleos"at the workplace or neighbourhood levelS where the party rank and file participate in discussion and IN organizing work. Although the party has experienced set-backs and disappointments in its quest for the presidency, it now has mayors in 187 cities, 56 federal deputies, 5 senators and governors in 3 states.

National Vote for the PT in Congressional Elections

	% of votes	No. of seats in the Chamber of Deputies	No. of seats in the Senate
1982	1.8	8	0
1986	3.2	16	0
1990	7	35	1
1994	9	49	5
1998	9.5	56	5

Updated from Branford and Kucinski, *Brazil: Carnival of the Oppressed*
(London: Latin American Bureau, 1995), p. 74.

NOT JUST AN ELECTORAL MACHINE — THE RELATIONSHIP
BETWEEN PARTY AND SOCIAL MOVEMENTS

The PT emerged from below with a strong working class base and a substantial proportion of its leadership drawn from the labour movement. However, the PARTY has no formal institutional links with the unions.[9] "Nor have the unions ever controlled it, or even funded it. To remain a broadly-based party the PT has allowed other social groups, such as landless peasant families and state employees, a large say in running the party. Its militants are active in most mass-based movements in Brazil, and lead many of them, but these movements have no formal place in the party structure and frequently clash with municipal governments run by the PT."[10] It is significant to note that the party maintains an 'organic' relationship with the social movements, which remain autonomous, and that only individuals can affiliate with the party. It is also noteworthy that the PT has not abandoned its working class base but has gradually become more inclusive - putting more emphasis on broad questions of citizenship and social justice and local issues with multi-class appeal.[11]

The PT has never been just an electoral machine. "For its militants, the PT is more than just a party; it is a lifestyle, a meeting point, a culture: the PT is the 'let's party party,' as many activists acknowledge."[12] Not only are they helping to lead popular struggles, they are actively developing a new culture, a 'way of being' more than an ideology.[13] Quite self-consciously, they cast an image of themselves as a happy, modern, and youthful movement in contrast to the stiff, old-fashioned parties. They've attracted a whole host of avant-garde cultural producers - TV and theatre actors, radio personalities, musicians, journalists, writers, cartoonists, graphic artists, architects and fine artists. They ensure that their "brand" - the red star - is everywhere - on t-shirts, buttons, stickers, posters, umbrellas, diaries, and even CD holders. They invent slogans on a daily basis and quickly disseminate them via posters and stickers. Their TV programs have a reputation for being funny.   They make very active use of the Internet - check out their webpages and chatrooms at www.pt.org.br. And their young militants wear images of Che Guevara, keeping him very much alive in Brazil.

What are the ideas behind this party that make it so dangerous? It offers a radical mix of democracy and citizen participation. It maintains a strong base in the grass-roots social movements and is a militant advocate for the rights of workers, of women, of cultural and ethnic minorities, for the environment and a host of other social causes. It remains active between elections - organizing protests and supporting workers on strike.[14]   It encourages different viewpoints within its ranks rather than impose one monolithic ideology. Perhaps more important, when it wins political office it uses its power to improve living conditions for the mass of people.

Although PT governments still have to manage within a capitalist economy, they have shown considerable courage in questioning the neo-liberal model. To cite but one example, the Governor of

Rio Grande do Sul challenged the previous government's commitment to give tax breaks and government loans to Ford and General Motors to create factories in his state. Such inducements would have cost hundreds of millions of dollars that had been earmarked for the salaries of public employees, and for health, education and other essential infrastructure. Although Ford withdrew in order to accept incentives from a rival state, the governor was vindicated by public opinion, which put a higher priority on improving public services than giving aid to transnational corporations.[15]

PT - OPEN, DEMOCRATIC AND PLURAL

The PT defines itself in three words: open, democratic and plural. Openness was demonstrated at the outset, when the party accepted people from a variety of left-wing groups, each of which hoped to shape the party towards its point of view. This encouraged a climate of intensive internal debate and a vibrant pluralism of ideas. At the same time, the party has remained open to popular movements and has taken on new issues such as the environment, culture and sexuality. Dozens of "tendencies" continue to exist within party. Although the factionalism can be wearing, it helps overcome the anonymity of membership in a mass party - most can find an ideological affinity group where they are welcome and comfortable. In fact, the party ensures that a plurality of opinions continue to be heard within its decision-making structures, and avoids electing "slates" whereby the winning faction takes all the seats. The results are exciting. According to Veja, a Brazilian news magazine, "The PT has something that the other parties lack - life. In the PT, you will find debate, contradictions, self-sacrificing militants, new ideas."[16]

What is the ideological glue that keeps this party together? As Branford and Kucinski explain, "it is not a particular definition of socialism, far less a specific recipe on how to achieve it, but an ethos, an attitude towards society and political involvement that combines radicalism, self-denial and moral outrage."[17] This stands in stark contrast to Brazil's political culture of self-interest, and helps to explain why the PT has not acted opportunistically, seized short-term political gains, or engaged in political horse-trading. The party stands for morality in politics, prompting their adversaries to lambast them for attitudes of self-righteous moral superiority.

In summary, the Workers Party is neither a traditional vanguard party, a social democratic party, or a green party, but all of these together.[18] The PT has been described as more of a social movement than a traditional party. It often works in alliance with other political parties. Rather than trying to seize state power, the party is gaining power via popular participation.

THE PARTICIPATORY BUDGET PROCESS

Certainly the most dangerous idea offered by the PT is that it asks people how they want their taxes to be spent. The participatory budget process developed in Porto Alegre is now a model being studied around the world.[19] The city administration offers citizens the chance to express their needs through an elaborate series of town hall meetings and consultative structures. The city facilitates meetings in its sixteen regions and in five 'thematic' sectors such as health, education, and transportation. Investments are decided on the basis of a formula that takes account of three criteria: 1) the chosen priority of the region, whether it be sewage, pavement or education, etc; 2) the population of the region; and 3) the relative lack of services or infrastructure.[20]

Within each of these regions, a Regional Plenary Assembly meets twice a year. At the first meeting in March, the city government presents a report on how it has implemented the previous year's budget. The residents elect delegates to work out the spending priorities for the region, and smaller meetings are held in each neighbourhood over the next three months. Then the delegates report the local priorities to a second Regional Plenary, which ratifies the regional priorities and elects two delegates and substitutes to the city-wide Participatory Budgeting Council.

This Budgeting Council meets at least once a week over the following five months, from July to September, to formulate a budget for the whole city. It includes not only the two delegates elected from each of the regional assemblies, but two delegates elected from each of the five thematic plenaries, plus a delegate from the municipal workers union, one from the union of neighbourhood associations, and two delegates from central municipal agencies. By September 30th, they submit a proposed budget to the Mayor, who can either accept it or call for revisions. The Council can accept his amendments or over-ride his/her veto with a 2/3rds vote.

Participatory budgeting has three objectives: first, to have citizens participate directly in decisions about the management of the city and the development of their local area; secondly, to develop the political awareness and power of the citizens and their organizations; and thirdly, to build a genuinely democratic political culture.[21]

People do participate - even poor people find their opinions matter - and they can help dictate whether the city builds sewers, streets, parks or playgrounds. City officials estimate that 100,000 people, or eight percent of the adult population, participated in the process in 1996, including roughly 1000 groups or associations.[22] As a myriad of studies indicate, this process is proving to be efficient, open and transparent, accountable, honest and productive - it offers more sewers and more day-care. The process is now being copied in over 70 other cities, including Sao Paulo, and at the state level.

WHAT NEXT?

Long-time PT leader Lula da Silva is currently front-runner for the next presidential election in 2002, but no one should be over-confident. Cardoso's government has not been able to forestall the gathering economic crisis, which certainly raises the prospects for a PT victory. But the IMF still acts as gate-keeper, and PT politicians are having to make the trek to Washington to reassure the powers-that-be that they can be trusted with the reigns of power. Nonetheless,

> What the PT's growth shows is that the current conventional wisdom in the First World is absurd, particularly when seen from the south. The "end of history" is not at hand; capitalism has not triumphed over socialism; and the International Monetary Fund's recipe for unequal economic growth is not the only path to development open to the Third World.[23]

What next? The Workers Party is intent on offering a basic income to alleviate poverty and develop the citizenship potential of the very poor. The centrepiece of its campaign for the upcoming federal elections in 2002 is the promise of a "citizens wage," which means raising the minimum wage enough to lift people out of poverty.

Are these ideas really dangerous? They are not about collective ownership of the means of production. But they could have revolutionary implications if the Brazilians elect the Workers Party and the new government refuses to play the neo-liberal game, if they set social standards which put the well-being of their citizens first. Perhaps the best alternative to neo-liberalism will be found in struggle, as people simply say no and raise the bar, refusing to privilege the rights of international investors.[24]

NOTE

Special thanks to Carlos Torres for introducing me to the PT and Porto Alegre, to Daniel Schugarensky for refining my analysis, and to Glauco Araujo for checking my facts and increasing my appreciation of the PT.

[1]The first and by now classic accounts of the PT are by Emir Sader and Ken Silverstein, *Without Fear of Being Happy: Lula, the Workers Party and Brazil* (London and New York: Verso, 1991) and Margaret Keck, *The Workers' Party and Democratization in Brazil* (New Haven and London: Yale University Press, 1992). Sue Branford and Bernardo Kucinski offer a somewhat more up-to-date and less academic account in *Brazil: Carnival of the Oppressed: Lula and the Brazilian Workers Party* (London: Latin American Bureau, 1995).

[2]Huw Beynon and José R. Ramalho, "Democracy and the Organization of the Class Struggle in Brazil," *Working Classes, Global Realities*, Leo Panitch and Colin Leys (eds), (London: Merlin, 2000) p.220.

[3]As Branford and Kucinski testified in 1995, "Poverty in Brazil is not only relative but absolute. According to government figures, about 20 million people, out of an economically active population of 63 million, are either unemployed or earn less than the minimum wage of US $70 a month. Including these people's dependents, this means that there are roughly 70-80 million Brazilians - about half the population - who are too poor to give their children an adequate upbringing. According to some economists, about 32 million of this deprived population suffer from chronic malnutrition." op.cit.

[4]Boaventura de Sousa Santos, Boaventura de Sousa Santos, "Participatory Budgeting in Porto Alegre: Towards a Redistributive Democracy," *Politics and Society* 26:4 (December 1998), p.462.

[5]Walter Young, *The Anatomy of a Party: The National CCF, 1932-61* (Toronto: University of Toronto Press, 1969).

[6]Branford and Kucinski, op.cit., p. 4.

[7]Beynon and Ramalho, op.cit., pp. 230-233.

[8]Sader and Silverstein, op.cit., p. 157.

[9]The "new unionists" who created the PT in 1980 were also instrumental in forming a new 'Cental Union of Workers' (CUT) in 1983....

[10]Branford and Kucinski, op.cit., p.7.

[11]Ibid.

[12]Branford and Kucinski, op.cit., p.12.

[13]Workers Party of Brazil, *Paths*, Sao Paulo: Fundacao Perseu Abramo, 1999.

[14]PT supporters proudly note that "the PT parties the whole year" - not just at election time.

[15]Carlos Castilho, "Economy-Brazil: Workers Party Governor Locks Horns with GM, Ford," Inter Press Service, April 5, 2000. See also Michael Lööwy, "A 'Red' Government in the South of Brazil," *Monthly Review*, November 2000.

[16]Quoted in Branford and Kucinski, p.5.

[17]Ibid., p.10.

[18]In the works of Michael Lowy, "What is at stake here is a new type of party whose significance and interest extend beyond Brazil. It is not a matter of a social democratic party directed by parliamentarians, organized as an electoral machine with the usual neo-Keynesian reformist program and Atlanticist orientation. Nor is this a bureaucratic communist party with its omnipotent apparatus, its political and ideological submission to the USSR; it is not a populist party, such as Peronism or the old Partido Trabalhista Brasileiro (PTB - Brazilian Labour Party), directed by charismatic bourgeois politicians with a vaguely nationalist program and corrupt bureaucracy of "yellow" labour union political bosses. Finally, it is not a self-styled revolutionary sect, organized on the margins of real workers' movements and bound up in dogma and rigid rituals. In reality, it is difficult to find analogues and equivalents., "The Brazilian PT," *Latin American Perspectives* (Fall 1987) p.454, quoted in Sadler and Silverstein, op.cit. p.3.

[19]There is a growing literature about the participatory budget process. See, for example, Rebecca Abers, *Inventing Local Democracy: Grassroots politics in Brazil* (Boulder, Co: Lynne Reinner Publishers, 2000); Gianpaolo Baiocchi, "Participation, Activism, and Politics: The Porto Alegre Experiment in Deliberative Democratic Theory," in *Deepening Democracy: Institutional Innovations in Empowered Participatory Governance*, Archon Fung and Erik Olin Wright (eds), (forthcoming from Verso Press, 2002 - and available in manuscript at the Real Utopias website: http:www.ssc.wisc.edu/~wright); Daniel Schugarensky, "Grassroots democracy: the Participatory Budget of Porto Alegre," *Canadian Dimension*, 35 (1), Jan/Feb 2001; and Boaventura de Sousa Santos, "Participatory Budgeting in Porto Alegre: Towards a Redistributive Democracy," *Politics and Society* 26:4 (December 1998) 461-510.

[20]Vincent Pang, "The Experience of the Participative Budget in Porto Alegre,

Brazil" http://www.unesco.org/most/southa13.htm

[21]Daniel Chavez, "Cities for People," *Red Pepper* (June 1999) http://www.redpepper.org.uk

[22]Fung and Wright, op. cit. p.12.

[23]Sader and Silverstein, op.cit., p. 5.

[24]On a final note, there never were any mad cows in Brazil, but the Brazilian people became quite mad at the Canadian Government's high-handed actions in banning the import of Brazilian beef. Most regarded this act as another blow in the trade war between Canada and Brazil over their aircraft industries. Perhaps the Brazilians may still be angry enough to scuttle the Free Trade Agreement of the Americas, as they have threatened to do. They have been given a good taste of how these agreements work and whose interests they serve.

The Abundant Life For All:
The Heart of the Social Democratic Promise

ARMINE YALNIZYAN

I. THE VISION OF PROGRESS

SOCIAL DEMOCRATS, AND THOSE MORE BROADLY within left politics, whether in Canada or elsewhere, have held a certain consistent ideal vision of society over time. It is derived from the Judeo-Christian tradition, a tradition that is thousands of years old, an oral and written tradition that has reinterpreted the central story of the progressive vision in its teachings over and over again. The story is about "the abundant life for all". This simple phrase is crammed with ideas, invoking a quest for material comfort and pleasure, respect for individual and collective human rights, growth of personal potential, and a life rich with meaning and connectivity.

Over thousands of years, Western civilizations have made indisputable progress in bringing more abundance, in every sense, to an expanding sphere of society.[1] But still the search for the abundant life is far from over, both in the so-called developed nations and in those struggling to survive.

The reason why the story bears retelling throughout history, in the many parables and spiritual teachings, is because the search for the abundant life itself contains within it a profound tension, one that keeps pulling us off course, as it always has throughout history. We are pulled off course whenever:

1) abundance is framed only by the materialistic

2) the role of economic growth (and consequently markets) is overemphasized as the chief means of progress towards a "better life" for society

3) the primary tool for an individual to achieve the goal of the better life, the abundant life, is the labour market

4) cultural trends emerge that reduce the resonance of aspirational language, so that it becomes harder to remind and inspire people of the greater vision of progress, and easier to limit mainstream thought to the three myopic (and misguided) visions of progress, listed above

Throughout history, the search for abundance has been set in a context in which life's material necessities were tenuous for the majority of people. The search, therefore, has a distinctively material element to it. But the poetic call to an abundant life is not guaranteed only by achieving an abundant material life. The call to the abundant life beckons with something ultimately more satisfying than the elusive satisfactions of ever more stuff. At the individual level, the tension, or irony, in this call is that since it is not primarily about stuff, it is possible for even those without much material wealth to experience this abundance.

Nonetheless, there is some material threshold that must be reached for life to be abundant, otherwise life is simply a scramble for survival. So there is clearly some relationship between one's material station in life and how abundant one's life can be, and this leads to the call for a better life for all.

Though seemingly universal, this call actually places the focus on the poor, who are least able to achieve sufficiency in their means of survival. The centrality of this aspect of the call is painfully obvious today. Even with the unparalleled prosperity and unprecedented wealth such as Canada enjoys at this time, there is no natural mechanism to ensure that the most basic provisions, such as adequate shelter, food and clean water, exist for all citizens. So the second tension, or irony, in the call for a better life is at the collective level: simply attaining ever-increasing material abundance in a society (economic growth) does not automatically guarantee sufficiency for all, even at the most basic material level.

The world continues to become increasingly commodified over time, bringing the reach of the market deeper and deeper into the way we think about our lives.[2] The reverse image has shadowed this process, decreased reliance on community or extended family nexus, resulting in a growing number of individuals who struggle to attain sufficiency.

Historically, the great leap in the articulation of social rights was the right to revenue, as a means to accessing sufficiency. The right to revenue is not a passive right. It is a right only inasmuch as it is achieved through paid work, and that access to paid work is held as an important social goal. It is in this sense that full employment became the key social right of the post- war period. And it is in this sense that paid work, and consequently the labour market, became articulated as the key mechanism for achieving full citizenship.

The central social right - the right to engage and participate in one's own life, the right to development and growth of the human potential - was thus eclipsed by a derivative right, the right to access earning opportunities in the labour market.   Without access to income, primarily through the labour market, how can the fuller engagement and development of the human potential flourish? But it is easy to confuse means with ends.

As societies become increasingly framed and constructed by market exchanges, it becomes easier to put increasing emphasis on the translation of "the abundant life" on to material wealth. It is from there a short step to such inverted logic as "trickle down" theory to claim that the path to a more abundant life is to give more to those who already have more, in order that they create a bit more for those at the bottom. This leads us directly into the conundrum about the role of growth in society.

II. THE ROLE OF GROWTH

In economics, we are taught there is a trade-off between equity and efficiency, both being the object of progress in the most generous reading of the literature. Efficiency can be interpreted to mean; a) doing better with the scarce resources we have, with the premium on conservation or higher productivity of the factors of production; or b) making more, either more quantity or more profit, with the premium on growth. It is the latter definition of efficiency that has come into vogue, with a near-fetish about economic growth that relies, as its moral underpinning, on the idea that more growth will make life better for everyone.

Mainstream economic theory would have us believe interventions that move societies towards a more equal distribution of incomes and wealth impede efficiency, since investments of "significant" scale require concentration of resources. Because economic growth is posed as the mechanism to achieve the abundant life for all, it follows that we should not worry about greater inequality because there is a direct inverse relationship between equality and more stuff - more equality will slow down the rate of creating more stuff; less equality will speed it up. And, the reasoning goes, we will all be the beneficiaries if there is more money and more stuff in the system.

Economist Lars Osberg has documented, empirically, that there is no definitive case for a trade-off between growth and equality. Fast growth is coincident with both more and less equal societies. The corollary holds too. Greater equality is not achieved only in periods of economic growth.

The evidence for Canada in the 1990s, shows growth was not the magic bullet that led to greater equality. Government policies were.[3] Between 1989 and 1994, a period of economic recession, inequalities in earned incomes exploded, but after-tax income inequality actually lessened. Quebec, Ontario and British Columbia raised minimum wages and rates of social assistance at the turn of the decade, reducing inequality just as market forces were increasing it. Those changes were enough to tilt the balance, and put Canada on the map internationally as one of a handful of nations that did not fall into the lock-step of globalization, with its attendant growth in income inequality.

In the period 1994 to 1997, the reverse occurred. Economic growth kept accelerating and government policies that lessened income inequalities were cut back. Inequalities in earned income grew smaller, primarily because more people found work or increased their hours of work. But after-tax inequalities grew at a more rapid rate than had been documented since Statistics Canada started collecting the data. Again, it was government intervention that tilted the balance, with welfare cuts and UI cuts eroding incomes at the bottom, and tax cuts primarily accruing income to the top. Indeed, the two provinces whose economic rates of growth were the strongest - Ontario and Alberta - saw the most dramatic increase in income inequality; whereas the provinces with less robust economic growth either maintained or reduced after-tax income inequality.

Consistently over the past decade, the main message has been that the market is not only the best, but fundamentally the only way to assure enough for everyone. The evidence, however, points to the fact that the role of the market in improving everyone's lives is being over-emphasized, and the role of government is being under-emphasized.

By haggling over which sector is best equipped to deliver conditions favourable to rapid economic growth, a more important question is overlooked - that of the objective itself.

Growth is almost universally seen as the primary objective for governments and markets alike. To question this as the true goal of human effort risks being type-cast a Luddite or worse, even among those on the left.

The current nature of growth, however, itself dictates that the pursuit of deeper social goals, such as universal public education and improvements in health care, are relegated to a distant second place in defining the public good, even when the economy is growing.

The dominant model of growth has itself changed dramatically in the past two decades. Today, growth is predicated on a modality of organization and resource allocation that creates growing insecurity - in the labour market, and in financial markets (not to mention in the markets for food, shelter and water).

In the "golden age" of economic growth, roughly between the late 1950s and very early 1970s, economic growth meant rising wages and incomes, as well as increases in access to public goods. There was both an expectation and a commitment, on the part of governments and on the part of people, that life would truly get better for the individual household, no matter how modest.

During that phase of rapid economic growth, massive public investments were made, with the blessing of the "taxpayer". We collectively undertook the building of hospitals, universities and colleges, electrical utilities, public transport systems and highways, public swimming pools and recreational facilities. We supported and paid for the introduction of new universal programs to increase security. The economic ruin that could befall anyone who was sick, retired or unemployed was staved off by the establishment of Medicare and the public pension system, the significant expansion of Unemployment Insurance system, and the initiation of a cost-shared way of dealing with social assistance through the Canada Assistance Plan.

All this has been reversed during this latest period of economic growth. Rapid economic growth is coincident with virtually every public support listed in the paragraph above coming under the knife of "fiscal prudence". More troubling, rapid economic growth has come with more, not less, economic insecurity for a growing number of workers. As per capita income has grown, inequality in its distribution has grown apace.

The past two decades have seen the size of the economic pie almost double.[4] This same period has also been witness to steady loss of permanent, full-time, middle-income jobs as downsizing has become the central theme of corporate re-organization, in both public and private sector institutions. Enterprises pare down to their "core" activities in-house, and either out-source component production or spin off non-core functions. Labour-saving technologies play a role, too, in shedding labour from the work that needs to be done and increasing the competition for paid work.

Among the jobs that have replaced these lost employment opportunities, the most rapid growth has been in part-time, seasonal, contract and casual employment. The expansion of self-employment in the 1990s has been unprecedented in the post-war period. By the year 2000, 16% of the labour market was based on jobs created by the workers themselves. Data from Statistics Canada's Labour Force Survey show that when all the various forms of precarious employment are added (seasonal, contractual and other non-permanent employment, part-time employment, and self-employment) they accounted for just under half the work force (about 45%) in the year 2000.

The insecure labour market affects everyone, even those with regular full-time employment. But those on the front lines of this aggressively "just-in-time" deployment of labour are disproportionately represented by those aged under 35, and those newly arrived in Canada. It is no longer the reserve army of labour that produces the pressure on the employed to reduce their expectations. It is built into the very nature of being "increasingly productive", i.e. increasingly profitable. To borrow a phrase from the world of computer programming - garbage in, garbage out.

This phase of economic growth is predicated on growing insecurity. It should come as no surprise if it then delivers growing insecurity.

People's jobs are perhaps even more vulnerable today, during a period of remarkable economic growth, than they were twenty years ago during an economic recession. This is as true for those working in successful enterprises as those deemed in "sunset" industries, as true for upper level management as for those at the bottom of the workplace hierarchy. During this period of economic growth there are more people whose housing is precarious, who go hungry, and whose communities have unsafe drinking water.

In short, the necessities for living the most simple existence are less, not more, assured for a growing number, notwithstanding the fact that this is one of the most "advanced" countries the world has known, and that its economy is growing at the fastest rate in a generation. So it is not irrelevant to raise doubts about the centrality of economic growth as the key social project that we should all rally behind.

While nobody is arguing for a recession, not every type of economic growth creates the world we want. This is not an anti-growth position. It simply asks the question: what kind of growth and growth at what cost, to whom?

III. TOOLS FOR PROGRESS

Are these new problems? In a sense, they are absolutely new. At no time in the history of civilization have societies seen the co-existence of such abundance side by side with such lack of access to the very basics of life.

But these are also ancient problems. How to provide the basics for everyone is the oldest human story there is, the struggle between the ascendance of the individual or of the community. This is the conflict at the heart of the ideologies that swirl around us today in the messages from the political Right and the political Left.

To focus on the growing gap in incomes seems like a losing battle in the current political culture, when the only way of engaging discussion with the mainstream about incomes is to talk about income taxes and how we can get rid of them. This is clearly of no consequence to the approximately one-third of tax filers that pay no taxes at all in Canada and to their dependents.

More importantly, however, a movement towards a more equitable distribution of income is not the only important political ground to claim in the battle for a more just society. Even if one achieved progress towards this goal - and progress, not ultimate equality, is all that would be achieved - the basic costs of living are poised to rise far more quickly than incomes could hope to increase at the bottom of the spectrum, precisely because of the forces at play in the nature of economic growth at this time.

A focus on universal access to the basics of life - food, shelter - could be ground zero for a 21st century progressive politics. In Canada, this would mean a public policy premium placed on the creation of decent affordable housing and quality-assured water in every region of the country. (In this country, food security is almost exclusively a function of the proportion of household income going to shelter. If public policy got the housing/income relationship right, a natural by-product would be more money for food, in the vast majority of precarious households.)

But as far as we are from this objective in our "advanced" "world-class" country, it is also true that most Canadians are way beyond this reality. What vision of the abundant life can a progressive politics realistically offer them? A politics which speaks to a core of stability in an ever more insecure world. A politics people can rely on in times of need and when it is time to invest in the future. High quality, universally accessible public education and health care, child care, home care, and pharmaceutical care are also vital to the full development of individuals, communities and economies. In large urban centres, where Canadians increasingly reside, public transportation systems are critical to the efficient running of a city, for the mobility of its people and their needs, as well as the protection of its environment.

Finally, the progressive platform has, for far too long, been silent about the role of time in our lives. There is less and less attention paid to the time people need to rest, to restore themselves. Our personal lives are relentlessly intense. We have accepted an unnatural level of intensity in the way we do everything, from the way we farm and the way we use our natural resources. Not even the land is allowed to rest. In a world that is increasingly a 24-7 proposition, there is no allowance made for stopping, letting land lie fallow. Even naturally growing to maturity is too slow, as agribusinesses boost the rate of growth of fish and other animals with hormones.

The scriptures are explicit on the need for rhythm, for cadence, for balance between the competing claims of production and reproduction (that is, preparation for production) on our world, our lives. What emerges from these ancient texts is a clear and contemporary progressive platform, one that ties issues of sustainable development and working time into the search for abundance for all.

The growing gap in incomes is at least in part derived from growing inequalities in paid hours of work. Among those who still have full-time full-year employment, unpaid overtime is increasingly the handmaiden to the era of downsizing. With cutbacks to public services, fundraising and community involvement of all descriptions make ubiquitous pleas for our time.

Time is one of the last "commodities" whose value has not been fully demarcated in currency, and whose importance is systematically undervalued as it relates to being a full, participating human being and citizen, complete with the need for time out.

The tools for achieving these goals - basics for all, more stability, more time - include a mix of straight-forward increases in public service, planning with and providing more resources to the voluntary and co-operative sector, increased "bulk buying", redistributing working time, and legitimizing more paid time for parenting, illness and learning.

These three elements of a progressive platform - basics for all, more stability, more time - are at once sustaining and profoundly radical. Radical because they move in the direction of decommodifying the way we live, at a time when there is so much momentum towards ever greater commodification. And sustaining, because they revitalize and legitimate all aspects of engagement in the human project: development or, if you will, growth in the way we relate to ourselves, one another, and where we live.

Subtly transforming the language of growth to work towards this goal is, and has been, the work of progressives in society. As Pope John Paul II wrote in 1991, "It is not wrong to want to live better. What is wrong is a style of life which is presented to be better when it is directed towards 'having' rather than 'being'." The progressive clarion call is a call to fuller being, not more stuff.

IV.   CULTURE SHAPES LANGUAGE

A few months ago on TVO, I saw Allan Gregg interview Anita Roddick, owner of the Body Shop chain of stores. She was describing an idea she had for working with an indigenous tribe in Brazil, marrying the concepts of fair trade and community economic development with cutting-edge consumption for those who search the ultimate beauty product. She told of interviews with the media that critiqued and attacked every aspect of her idea, both before it was operational and at every unexpected turn during the process of trying to make it functional. The goal of doing something that genuinely created something new and valuable for all ends of the market transaction was obscured.

Anita Roddick said this experience made her conclude that you couldn't aspire to things in public anymore. It had to be a proven success before you could refer to it. You had to anticipate everything that could go wrong and have an answer for it before you were given the credibility and support to make something new happen. For me, she put her finger on a key aspect of the tenor of our times: the death of aspirational language.

This death was further marked by a print ad that was circulating around the same time. Alcatel, makers of communication networks, put out huge ads showing Martin Luther King Jr. making his famous "I have a dream" speech, from the front and, computer altered, from the back. Gazing at his focussed countenance, one could almost hear the thrilling voice and the magic of his stirring words. The view from his back, however, totally disconnects us from what we know about that moment. Looking out from the Lincoln Memorial, the ad shows an empty Washington Square where a sea of bodies had actually been assembled on that August day in 1963. The tag line reads "For passion to inspire a nation, it has to reach a nation." Somehow, the emphasis on process - delivering the audience - and the equivalent de-emphasis of what actually happened that day diminished the greatness of the message. This remains the impact of that ad every time I look at it, even though Martin Luther King Jr.'s message still has the power to move today, even to an audience of one reading the text in the silence of his or her own personal space.

Those two events made me think about how difficult it is to be a progressive leader these days, one who is able to move people towards progress guided by a vision of that progress, a dream.

The romanticism and idealism of most of the resistance movements of the 20th century were not devoid of pragmatic alternatives. They soared, despite the odds, not because of the imminent do-ability of these projects but because of the dreams that propelled the campaigns. Think of the suffragettes, the Russian Revolution[5], the Spanish Civil War, the Resistance during World War Two, the Civil Rights Movement, perhaps even the women's movement of the 1970s.

Today, however, romanticism and idealism seem woefully outdated, impractical and out of place in our political optics. People long for leaders, but don't really expect anyone or any programme of action to be capable of rising above the foibles of being human. The passionate driving force behind so much political change has given way to an entrenched cynicism and hyper-realism that leaves little room for human weakness or failure.

If there is little hope for a re-emergence of the charismatic leader with staying power these days, there is plenty of hope for the resurgence of grassroots power. Indeed, the field is clear for the articulation of a clear left agenda, an agenda that has always talked about the power of the people. And throughout the country many are doing far more than just talking the talk now. They are walking the walk, and joining others who want to stroll, march and run to the same places. What fuels this hope for a better world?

The last great burst of political optimism I can remember was the late 1960s and the early 1970s. Political parties were slow, then as now, to reflect the newly emerging power that people felt, as individuals and as part of movements. A profoundly individualist era was blossoming, fuelled by the contagious spirit of liberation and personal growth. Ironically the Zeitgeist of the time, with its demand to break down the walls, barriers and rules that fetter the human spirit, spread just like a contagion to the arenas of finance and trade, the consequences of which now cause us to struggle with the very relevance of politics, resistance, and progressive agendas.

"Small is beautiful" was the ubiquitous slogan that celebrated independent and local solutions to local problems. It was perhaps the greatest contributor to the call for devolution and decentralization of government policies. It remains a potent argument against those who struggle for a more progressive role for nation-states, in the belief that this is the most effective counter-weight to the march of corporate globalization.

The other, equally potent manifestation of the zeitgeist of the time was transcendence, the spirit of rising above. Culture shaped language profoundly, then as now. Manifestations of this spirit ranged from the most prosaic and frequent call to "get high", to a quest for finding the higher ground, to the most ambitious message of the time: transcendental meditation, which was framed not just as a tool for individuals, but as a way of changing the collective consciousness if practiced widely enough.

Mahatma Gandhi professed that transcendental meditation could alter our daily view of the world so that real priorities emerged more effortlessly in our lives. That centering of spirit has the capacity to calm interactions with others, and build consensus more easily. Ghandi claimed that, if one in ten people practiced transcendental meditation (or prayer), the community in which they lived would be profoundly, and positively, affected.

That ratio, one in ten, is not far off from the proportion of the population that engages in and affiliates itself explicitly with a progressive electoral politics in Canada. And we know there are many more who are energetically progressive but just don't want to play with politics anymore.

If Ghandi is right, and what we do can affect the society we live in for better of worse, what if we practiced the progressive vision, daily and concretely in our actions and our words?

Our culture, so pressed for time and so immersed in the quest for immediate gratification, has little time for idealism or romanticism. Consequently the pool from which our potential leaders are drawn is less likely to respond to those arching images that can propel a generation forward. With fewer people able to think in, or resonate with, the language of aspiration, it is no surprise that there are fewer leaders that can inflame The Dream in our breasts with the "right" language.

Nevertheless, longing for a better world, not just a better life, is a wide-spread aspiration. While this timeless human longing is still relevant today, our culture jeers and mocks those who voice these impersonal desires. Those deemed most cool in our culture label those who want these kind of goals - rather than the goals expressed by "Who wants to be a Millionaire", "Survivor" and "Greed" - as hopelessly uncool and out of touch with what the modern world is about: winning, winning ever-more stuff. It's never enough. And you don't need leaders for that kind of winning.

Culture doesn't change over night. The continuous wash of these types of messages will have to be outweighed by a critical mass of messaging that is looking for something more than winning, winning more stuff. Until that rock reveals itself as the uneroded base for our times, we might do well to think of our individual words and actions as having the capacity to lead, if but for a moment, those around us. If our "leaders" cannot do the job, if there are no real leaders anymore, then it's up to us, all of us. We are the leaders now.

Whatever words we put to it, all of us on the left are somehow inspired by a vision of the abundant life, not for just some but for all. Each of us can champion some part of the journey in making progress towards that vision. That leadership of the many is, perhaps, the most vital way to breathe some life into the old dream again .... the dream of the abundant life - in the most mundane and the most poetic senses - for all.

---

[1]This paper is not intended to be xenophobic in any way. The reason that I approach the issue in this way is that I have insufficient direct knowledge of non-Western societies, and have no intimacy with teachings outside the Judeo-Christian heritage. My paper is based on what I know, not the totality of the historical framing of this issue.
[2]Commodification occurs when a process or relationship enters the domain of per unit exchange for money. For example, domestic services have become available for purchase by the unit, such as individual servings of food, housecleaning by the hour, part-time child or elder

care. Industrial polluters have created a market for trade in quotas for allowable amounts of emissions. There is a growing market in organs for transplants.

[3] See Armine Yalnizyan, *Canada's Great Divide*, Toronto: Centre for Social Justice, January 2000.

[4] GDP at market prices grew from $535 billion in 1980 to $921.5 billion in 2000, in inflation adjusted "constant" (1992) dollars. See Statistics Canada, Canadian Economic Observer, Catalogues 11-210-XPB (Historical Supplement) and 11-010-XPB (May 2001), Table 1 in each.

[5] I hesitantly include this in the list, as the Russian Revolution led directly, and not by mistake, to one of the most dictatorial and most brutal regimes the world has witnessed.

Is the Media Right?

MICHAEL VALPY

THE LEFT IN CANADA MUST FIND ITS OWN MEDIA VOICE. With that bald statement, a few words first on my understanding of journalism.

Many years ago when I was a young reporter, a new girlfriend took me to a lecture by the Australian mythologist P.L. Travers, better known as Pamela L. Travers, the creator of Mary Poppins. I knew next to nothing about mythology; my interest was in the new girlfriend. Travers spoke exquisitely, precisely, about a society's deepest values, its most profound self-images and goals, its truest voice - about all those things being expressed and shaped by myth. At the end of her lecture, I stood up and asked how a society's myths were transmitted in the present. Her answer was dismissive. "Don't you ever read your newspapers?" she said . . and went on to the next questioner, leaving behind someone — me — with the classic cartoon light bulb switched on over his head. At that moment I understood what I did for a living.

I am a mythologizer. My role as a journalist is not to pretend that I communicate pristinely objective information — information that doesn't exist, never has existed and never will exist. My role, as the late American social historian Christopher Lasch said, is to "enter into certain important conversations with the culture." I am Homer, Aesop, the Brothers Grimm with a hefty dash of Jung, identifying and telling stories that embody the values Canadians believe to be true about themselves or — and this is the ticklish part — identifying and telling stories that create an image of what Canadians *might like to believe* to be true about themselves.

This is what I do, what every journalist does, what every owner of a newspaper or radio or TV station does. We who create and produce the mass media are image-makers, selective messengers, behind-the-scenes carpenters of cultural narrative, picking good guys and bad guys, addressing through the prisms of our own beliefs — actually, overwhelmingly the beliefs of our managers and owners — the deepest patterns of meaning and coherence in our society.

History and mythology are two equally valid vehicles for informing a society about itself. Let me give an uncomplicated illustration.

History records ideas and events: Pierre Trudeau did X, Y and Z as prime minister (or maybe he didn't; political accomplishment exist in the eye of their media beholders). He died on Sept. 28, 2000, and most Canadians grieved, bathed for days in maudlin and entertaining media images.

Mythology records something "other," something more profound. It speaks to our minds beneath our minds. It is the delivery of idea and image at the same time, banging on both sides of our brain. It addresses beliefs and values. The death of Pierre Trudeau, our most deliberately mythological prime minister, evoked in many Canadians a deep, powerful reminder of the Canada he had tried to create, a Canada which they once believed to exist and wished they still had: the Canada of a Just Society, of collective caring, of confidence, uniqueness and unity, of principles and purpose, a Canada, gosh, even of excitement and style. It did not matter whether that Canada was ever "true." It was *believed* to be true — and of those beliefs the media said very little.

Indeed, if we look at the mass media images of Trudeau before he died, we find quite a different narrative. We find images of an antediluvian gaffer out of touch with the political realities of contemporary Canada and Quebec, an arrogant, wrong-headed welfare-state centralist who sank his country in public debt, draped the business community in chains, did his utmost to castrate the marketplace, stole the wealth of the West and rammed French down our throats while he simultaneously smashed the legitimate aspirations of *pur laine* Quebeckers. History? Or mass media mythologizing at full gallop — mainly the mythological image of Trudeau that the neoliberal corporate media owners (cheered by nationalists in Quebec and their power-hungry political counterparts in other provinces) wished to present to the country in their own self-interest and in the interests of their class.

As for "truth," Trudeau wasn't an antichrist socialist, or really much of a socialist of any sort. He did no more, and in many ways far less, than the leaders of social democratic governments in much of Europe. At the first fracture in the early 1970s of the postwar Keynsian economic consensus, he trashed his government's plan for a guaranteed annual income, thus ending further progress of the Canadian welfare state; certainly we never equalled the achievements of the Europeans. He lost interest in his so-called Third Option to steer Canada away from U.S. economic domination. He was no inflexible centralist: he abandoned his 1978 constitutional reforms in the face of provincial opposition; he later abandoned his cherished dream of a constitution-amending referendum that in the national interest could have overridden provincial vetoes. He only reluctantly accepted constitutional entrenchment of aboriginal treaty rights. He was unenthusiastic about opposing apartheid in South Africa (Canadians had to wait for Brian Mulroney for that to happen). He had little interest in foreign aid. Civil libertarians never forgave him for the War Measures Act. Really, if we want to fit Trudeau accurately into our national mythology, he was the two-faced Janus, a symbol of opposing mythologies, of opposing visions of the country. But only one of those visions achieved the stature of a mass media narrative, the narrative (largely) that had big money behind it.

The argument here is so straightforward as to be almost uninteresting.

Events and ideas are the property of history. But without full access to the mechanisms of narrative and image — mass media — people cannot tell or hear the stories that are important to what they may believe, may hope, to be true about those events and ideas.

They cannot tell or hear the stories that reside in their hearts about their society. They are made the prisoners, even the victims, of other people's narratives and images. They become voiceless, except as digits in a public opinion poll or Xs on a ballot, made pitiable in "human interest" stories or, with increasing frequency, demonized at demonstrations that have become the frustrated and angry new politics of the street. That is why the Left in Canada must find its own media voice. Not a propaganda sheet. Not a passel of well-meaning community newsletters. Not a merely a clutch of Internet 'Zines -- increasingly influential as they are — or the occasional well-timed comment-page article or published letter to the editor, or some prayerful reliance on sympathetic columnists and reporters or a blue-moon meeting with an editorial board. But a full-fledged, professional, high-standard, media voice.

And before I go on . . .

I once read an editorial in the Boston *Herald* that began: "The success of the Left, despite the instinctive conservatism of the American people, is based on its control of society's idea generators — academia, the news media, Hollywood and book publishing." Yes, and Conrad Black, now departed from Canada to obtain nobility in Britain's House of Lords, has said the mass media in Canada are in the thrall of weedy leftists. I've been reading stuff like that my entire journalistic life. It is not reality.

My personal political and social beliefs have been no secret over nearly 30 years to the editors-in-chief of *The Globe and Mail*, to the newspaper's readers or, I suppose since the 2000 federal election, to the country. *The Globe and Mail*'s most Red Tory editor, Richard J. Doyle, invited me onto the paper's editorial board and later appointed me its national political columnist. Its most neoliberal editor, William Thorsell, allowed me to write a rampant column for most of his watch, once telling me irritably that I had wound up with a mandate of political comment almost as broad as his own. Its current editor, Richard Addis, readily allowed me leave of absence to run as an NDP candidate and welcomed me back from partisan politics without hiding me in a closet. I like to think that means my journalism meets the standards of *The Globe and Mail*. It also means *The Globe and Mail* has allowed me — in periodic large chunks — a voice to create a narrative of events. For which I am appreciative. It is not my newspaper. It is Bell Globemedia Publishing Inc.'s newspaper.

But that's the point: it's not my newspaper. And crumbs, scraps, a snack do not add up to every day's mass media full-meal. A Rick Salutin and a Naomi Klein here, a Linda McQuaig there, a Dalton Camp, a Joey Slinger and a Thomas Walkom somewhere else are no balance to the full mass media's commanding narrative of events of the world — to what's known as the news agenda: the front page headlines and stories, the lead items on the national television and radio news broadcasts, the mass media's selective focus on events and personalities and ideas (plus the insidious element of pack journalism, the collegial chorus) that reflect the spin of political elites and the interests of corporate elites and daily flood the world of Canadian political discourse. This is not paranoia. In the words of the late Richard Hatfield, former premier of New Brunswick: "Some of your enemies are your enemies." It is *their* newspapers, *their* radio and television stations, at a moment of one of history's major transformational periods, a period characterized by Christopher Lasch as the revolt of the elites — the abdication of the well-off, the well-educated, the most fortunate beneath the rubric of globalization from societal responsibility to the least fortunate, to the losers — and, indeed, to the broad middle class.

The evidence of mass media's complicity in the elites' revolt is pervasive. The evidence of its support for the commanding ideology of neoliberalism is overwhelming. The evidence of its declaration that no alternative exists — or existed (its conviction is not as sure as it once was) — to neoliberalism is not in question.

Where does one find, as a for-instance, the balance in mass media between reporting on government deficits and tax reduction on the one hand and, on the other, reporting on the continuing extensive damage to social programs and the hurt suffered by so many Canadians over the past two decades? Why isn't Canada's affordable housing crisis a day-by-day media outrage full of images of Parliament Hill scrums with reporters demanding answers from accountable ministers? Why does the fraud of the proclaimed federal-provincial agreement to reform primary health care and open the door to pharmacare not find a regular place on the news agenda? Why doesn't the media, with all the power it possesses, not daily trumpet the effects — on our air, our water, our natural spaces, the other creatures with whom we share this land — of the national government's appalling environmental record and its jellied response to provincial resistance? Why do the annual deaths of 5,000 Canadians due to air pollution not merit a high rank on the news agenda?

Why has there been, in the media, such a diminution and debasement of public institutions, so little objection to the encroachment of the market on public space (except in moments of disaster, like a Walkerton)? Where are the media's investigative reporters sniffing out the locations of the national government's secret plots of genetically modified wheat that are being grown over the fruitless objections of farmers and the government's own Canadian Wheat Board? Where are the media protests against the epidemic corporatization of university research?

Where is the media's insistence on true transportation alternatives to the automobiles that soil our air and blot our urban landscapes? Where is the media questioning why money exists for the rebuilding of Toronto's airport — the transportation mode of the global business world — but not Toronto's crumbling and inadequate public transit system — the transportation mode of ordinary workers? Why has the media let the Ontario Harris government get away for years with dumping the full cost of public transit on Toronto, the only major urban area on the continent forced to support its own transit system without support from other levels of government? Where, in general, are the media's demands for urgent provincial and federal government attention to our cities, the engines of the new global economy? How has our national Liberal government got away with pretending cities don't exist, while other national governments — including that of the United States — recognize that the success of their cities means the success of their national economies in a highly competitive world, and are pouring billions of dollars into urban transit, housing, public schools and other municipal infrastructure? Why, incidentally, does the media so complacently accept that the only measurement of an economy's health is the value of goods and services bought and sold, and not the costs downloaded onto the environment, not the costs to people without adequate housing, without adequate (or any kind of) jobs, not the costs downloaded onto publics who subsidize the airports and highways and other infrastructures that enable the market to function?

Where is the state of democracy on the news agenda? Why does the surrender of Canadian sovereignty to undemocratic trade organizations not have pride of place on the front pages and lead items of the newscasts? Where are the media reports about trade department bureaucrats secretly vetting government regulations before they are gazetted to ensure that they comply with international trade rules — meaning Canadians now don't know what regulatory protections they're *not* getting and *can't* have because of international trade pacts? Why do those who protest against this undemocratic loss of sovereignty, against corporate global despoliation of the environment, against corporate global erosion of human dignity find themselves characterized in the media as "the young and the witless," as people who speak for no one but themselves? Why are the politics of the street denigrated, indeed criminalized in the media? Why does this happen, while, with little more than a raised eyebrow from the media, the entire downtown of a major Canadian city is sealed off — a shocking affront to the constitutional guarantee of freedom of assembly — for a meeting of hemispheric heads of governments to talk about trade, and Canadian corporate leaders are invited to pay money to have access to them? On that last subject, when was the last time the media investigated who has more ready access to government: the Business Council on National Issues or the Canadian Labour Congress, the Canadian Manufacturers Association or the Canadian Environmental Law Association? Where are the demands from the media that it should be a matter of public record who a cabinet minister sees? Why does the media accept so readily that Parliament and provincial legislatures have become empty shells for their respective executives? Why did the media accept Stockwell Day's rise to the leadership of the Canadian Alliance virtually without scrutiny — and only proclaim him to be a mistake with the debacle of his leadership staring Canadians in the face?

And where is the other narrative about 2001's "war against terrorism"? What different media images would be in the minds of Canadians if the newspapers, radio and television had given the same focus to the children dying in Iraq because of sanctions, to the wreckage of Iraqi families bombed — the same focus as that given to the people who suffered the terrible events in New York City and Washington? Where is the focus on the political and economic policies of the American Empire? Duke University's Stanley Hauerwas, described by Time magazine as the most provocative theologian in

America today, pointed out in a recent interview that most Americans, because of their media, aren't even aware that they live at the centre of an empire.

There's a journalistic maxim that says: "If you want to know the reason for something, ask who benefits." The media accepts, supports and cheerleads what is in the interests of the media's owners. It is their media; it is their narrative, their mythology.

There is another journalistic maxim that says: "It's easy to be a critic. It is easy to state, and restate, a problem; it is not easy to state a solution."

The Left does not have $190-million (apres Conrad Black) to sink into a newspaper in order tell its narratives and address the values of Canadians. The Left is not instantly, perhaps not even eventually, going to create a Canadian *Guardian*. Solutions lie in imagination, hard thought and the recognition of opportunity.

Maybe opportunities already have been missed. For example, the recent sale of Conrad Black's Hollinger newspapers may have been a chance to acquire a small daily with union funding and build it into a national voice through convergence with digital broadcasting and Internet technologies.

Let me offer an idea that has been circulated recently by Don LePan, president of Calgary's Broadview Press.

"No one on the left or centre-left," he says, "has indicated any possibility of marshalling the resources necessary to launch another full-scale newspaper. Intelligent readers can make a mental adjustment to filter out a great deal of the bias in what is reported in the press — but even the most intelligent of readers cannot compensate for the fact that, because of the right-wing bias of the mainstream press, a wide variety of issues receive little or no coverage."

At the same time, in most major Canadian cities and many smaller urban centres there exist one or two weeklies with a left, or centre-left, political orientation. Their prime purpose is to provide local arts and entertainment information, but many also report on local politics and even attempt coverage of national and international issues. Their readership is generally, but not exclusively, younger than traditional newspaper audiences. In most cases these weeklies rely solely on advertising and are given away, and they are, in fact, read by considerable numbers of people.

LePan's proposal is to create a new, national newspaper that would be an eight- or twelve-page insert in these weeklies. It would be made available to them electronically. It would be free of charge to any weekly signing on; revenue would be generated by the sale of advertising for the eight or twelve pages — pages, keep in mind, that would appear across the country and thus have a national audience.

The insert would have its own professional staff of journalists. It would be broadly left of centre. "It would be," says LePan, "counterproductive to make it exclusively or dogmatically [left]. If mainstream readers were to be attracted, it would be important to include independent and centrist points of view (and even the occasional right-of-centre voice) — in much the same way as the better mainstream newspapers (*The New York Times, The Globe and Mail*) find space for the occasional left-wing voice."

LePan states that such a newspaper could be established fairly quickly and at a fairly low cost — he suggests an initial capitalization of well under $1-million.

It is an idea. There undoubtedly are other ideas.

The events of Canada in the 21st century are common to everyone. It is the narratives and images of those events that differ, and this is a country with images and narratives that are not those of the owners of corporate media. With the world transforming, re-gelling, the Left will be left at the margin without a media to call its own.

TWO:

WHAT'S LEFT?
The New Democratic Party in Debate

Towards A Revitalized Federal Party

ALEXA MCDONOUGH

In 1939 my parents attended a CCF convention on their honeymoon. The passions associated with building a new party of the left sprang from the same source as that which brought this young couple together. For my parents, politics and life were one and the same. Yet 30 years later, the unity of public and private life proved untenable. As the Left's political fortunes waned and party resources dried up, my father, like others, was forced to end his romance with politics to attend to the family business.

It was at this juncture that I entered politics fuelled by the same passion that my parent's generation felt for this party. Ten campaigns later, the passion still survives but so do the dangers that have given our party its unwieldy electoral history. Even today, as party leader, I am often asked by anxious new democrats " What future does the Federal New Democratic Party of Canada have?"

During the summer of 2001, ten thousand Canadians, mostly New Democrats, but many not, participated directly in the post election "re-think". More meetings and events are scheduled in the run up to the federal convention in November. Tough questions have been asked. New ideas have been vigorously debated. I am increasingly confident that the 2001 convention will chart a course for greater social democratic electoral success. But, this will only happen if we face our challenges squarely and lay the foundation for major changes with an appropriate sense of urgency.

Certain key questions must be settled;
• are we serious about seeking political power?
• what ought to be the relationship between the federal party and the provincial parties?
• what is to be done in relation to Labour and in relation to the grassroots?
• how big a tent should we be occupying and how do we rekindle the social democratic imagination ?

I've spent most of the summer reviewing our party's history and considering our prospects for electoral success. I now wish to bring some of my conclusions forward.

THE ELECTORAL MISSION

There have always been political adversaries charging that the desire for power has killed the "movement" and that true democracy resides exclusively in political protest from "outside the fence". Those voices have been heard once again throughout the renewal process, insisting that the pursuit of political power is a sell out of democratic socialist principles. To take such a position is, in my view, to misconstrue the founders' purpose and to miss the whole point of our mandate. The Regina Manifesto and the birth of the CCF were launched in an unapologetic pursuit of political power "to put an end to the capitalist domination of our political life".

Nor should we be led astray by such questions as have become the mainstay of invidious pollsters: "Should the NDP play the role, federally, of a mainstream alternative with a social conscience, or should the NDP opt for a more distinct role representing interests like anti-globalization and the environment?" The very question is moot because the answer is clearly both. The majority of Canadians do not accept the threat of globalization and the concomitant loss of sovereign control. Most Canadians care about the environment and as a party we ought actively pursue and represent the interests of the majority of Canadians. After all these are our interests as well.

The unprecedented transfer of power from citizens to corporations, advocated by Canada's ruling party, the destruction of our ecosystem and the growing income gap, can only be reversed by challenging the abusers of power at the ballot box, and by offering concrete, practical solutions to Canadians' every day concerns.

Mainstream editorialists understand this. One of Nova Scotia's major dailies, the Halifax Herald, describes the NDP's current identity crisis as a preoccupation with whether the federal NDP should "abandon any pretense of ever forming the government, and focus instead on becoming an "effective protest party". The Halifax Herald inveighs against this preoccupation and strongly suggests that the NDP do its level best to form government.

"If there is an alternative agenda, of a compelling nature in Canada", wrote Lawrence Martin of the *Daily News*, "it is on the left where big issues such as globalization, the environment, water, corporations, and Canada as a entity distinct from the United States, offer fodder for a strong political party".

Democracy is central to our mission. New Democrats are justly proud of the role we've played in democratizing Canadian society. But today, democratic erosion is rampant and we need to elevate democracy to the level of an obsession! Revitalizing democracy will take big ideas and widespread activism. We must vigorously advocate and build popular support for proportional representation so that people's votes translate into parliamentary voices. We must advocate reform of election financing.

At our last convention, both the federal NDP and the CLC opened up the debate on banning corporate and union donations to political parties. Disallowing union contributions while the millions continue to pour into the coffers of the corporate-sponsored parties would amount to unilateral disarmament. To undertake such disarmament is madness. We should, however, campaign together for these reforms and keep the corporate-dominated parties on the defensive, reinforcing our role as the proto–democratic party. We need to continue challenging our opponents to operate with the exclusive support of our citizens.

We need to champion local democracy, support community economic development and participate in activist coalitions. We also need to recognize and respect the fact that most NGOs, social advocacy groups, and non-profits do not consider themselves free to affiliate, or even publicly associate, as organizations, with a political party. At the same time, we must seek ways "to bridge the yawning gap between grassroots activists and electoral politics" as CUPE National President and Renewal Steering Committee member, Judy D'arcy, put it. This means gently coaxing individual members of grassroots organizations to join the New Democratic Party. This in turn means that we must open up discussions on party building and policy development to their input. Change requires both parliamentary and extra-parliamentary work. These are not mutually exclusive arenas but parallel tracks and we must find ways of impressing young people with that undeniable truth.

As a Party, we need to adopt one-member, one-vote to attract new members and provide opportunities for more direct participation in leadership selection and key elements of decision-making. Political relationships, after all, are based on power, not theory, as Des Morton reminds us, and a political party that fails "to develop a strong and representative membership base will have only a feeble claim to influence the policy of even a sympathetic government."

FEDERAL/ PROVINCIAL RELATIONS

The election of provincial New Democrats to government sometimes strain relations within the Party as a whole. Invariably, our political rivals make the federal party pay dearly for mistakes and mis-steps of our provincial counterparts. This has led some people, including CCPA founder and Ottawa University professor Duncan Cameron, to suggest that the federal party should seek an amicable separation.

Over the next year we must negotiate a new relationship with our provincial sections. We need to constitute the federal party as a separate entity graduating from our current "weak sister" status. The objective is not to establish distance or disavow one another. On balance, we've benefited more than we've been penalized by our respective efforts. But the federal Party must develop a more independent identity in order to achieve a more effective, respectful partnership with the provinces.

The federal Party must develop a clearer pan-Canadian mandate and an international perspective, focused on strengthening global democratic structures to counter corporate globalization.

RECONSTRUCT THE LABOUR RELATIONSHIP

Immediately following the 2000 Federal election, the Canadian Labour Congress president, Ken Georgetti, announced a major review of the labour movement's partnership with the New Democratic Party. His comments about the NDP's failure to meet electoral objectives were candid, constructive, and welcome. As a federal party we need an open, frank and forward-looking dialogue about the nature of our future relationship.

In the 1995 leadership campaign, I strongly endorsed the solid partnership between the NDP and the labour movement. I still do. But we need to negotiate a new relationship with a chance of better electoral results.

Some labour activists regard "one-member, one-vote" as a potential threat to an effective labour-party partnership. My view is the opposite. Any formula for future electoral success needs to include direct participation by trade unionists in party building and decision-making, and a sense of ownership in the outcome.

I believe "one-member, one-vote" would also help to eliminate the resentment harboured by some union members who believe that the partnership with the Party exists in reality only at the leadership level.

We need to challenge ourselves to go out after, not only votes, not only financial contributions, not only party memberships, but the participation through direct membership of as many of the 2.5 million trade unionists in this country as can be persuaded to join the party.

When I first stated support for one-member, one-vote, I made it clear that this policy in no way precludes some form of direct representation of labour in the Party's governance structure. Many trade unionists have responded to one-member, one-vote with enthusiasm.

I'm more persuaded than ever of the merits of incorporating

one-member, one-vote into whatever new Labour-NDP relationship is negotiated in the coming months. That obviously is a matter for discussion and negotiation with careful attention to both principles and details.

Labour has been a key factor in NDP struggles and NDP successes. As stated in the recent CLC paper on labour and politics, "Politics is Everything We Do!" Party support at leadership levels has been nearly universal. Even greater participation in future, with commensurate representation, and greater transparency and accountability at all levels of decision making, would be to our mutual advantage.

BUILDING A BIGGER TENT

James Laxer, York University Political Science professor, recently suggested the party's goal should be to mobilize the majority of the population, made up of wage and salary earners, in opposition to the power exercised over them by corporations and the wealthy. With 65% of Canadians struggling financially, living from pay cheque to pay cheque, and discouraged about their financial situation the potential for expanding the tent, building a broader social democratic party, is enormous.

Through the Renewal process, many individuals have shared ideas on how to accomplish this expansion. Some Ad Hoc groups, such as NDProgress and the New Politics Initiative have advanced their formulae. Paul Hellyer of the Canada Action Party proposes that the CAP and the NDP reconstitute in one large, progressive nationalist party to attract Canadians who want to regain the decision-making transferred to NAFTA and the WTO, and preserve the social and cultural differences that make us distinctively Canadian.

With democracy under fire, corporations in control, and the environment in peril, we must succeed in our mission to build a bigger tent.

Party building is a time consuming, arduous process. Party ending is perhaps even more difficult. This is perhaps a compelling argument for simply reinventing, and reinvigorating the NDP! In these respects and despite twenty years as an elected politician I remain receptive to each and every option that promises to strengthen social democracy.

REVITALIZED NDP ROOTED IN SOLIDARITY

Whatever the form of Canada's renewed left, its foundation must be the social democratic values of equality, democracy, and sustainability. To that ineluctable inventory I would add a further value -solidarity, which is the substance that holds a healthy society together and gives it strength.

In June, I attended meetings of the Socialist International Council in Lisbon. It was the Fiftieth Year Anniversary of the Socialist International. S.I. President, Antonio Guterres, spoke of "building a society based on solidarity, the task of every State and a universal task in a globalized world."

As we push ahead with the task of reinventing the federal NDP and reinvigorating social democracy in Canada, we must ground our efforts in that same solidarity – not just in concept but in practice.

UNLEASH OUR SOCIALIST IMAGINATION

Bruce Wark, journalism professor at University of Kings College, argues that the NDP is facing problems today, not because the party's social democratic ideals are outdated, but because we need a fresh theoretical framework, a more *coherent* and credible "economic critique of production-oriented philosophies and their accompanying shrinking of the public space – especially in light of the worsening environmental crises." Wark's charge that the left's prescriptions seem partial and piecemeal is widely shared.

Steve Shrybman documents how free trade is "creating dynamics fundamentally at odds with any reasonable notion of sustainable development." This puts the challenge squarely to a party, which defines sustainability as one of its core principles, and the environment as a top priority.

Respected economist and Renewal Steering Committee member, Armine Yalnizyan, urges the federal Party to find a new socialist imagination. Over the past five years, I have shared the frustration felt by many that the intellectual vitality, the creative energy of the Federal NDP has waned. Many have said more bluntly, "We know what you're against, but what are you for?" We need to breathe intellectual life back into our politics. It is promising that people across the country have come forward during the renewal process offering their ideas, talents and expertise to flesh out practical, concrete policy alternatives. We need to tap into that brain trust, especially to develop a solid economic platform. We must utilize the new communications technologies that make it feasible and affordable to engage party members and the progressive public in an ongoing, interactive policy development process. The honey-moon is very far from over.

The New Politics Initiative:
Open, Sustainable, Democratic

JIM STANFORD & SVEND ROBINSON

WHO WE ARE

THE NEW POLITICS INITIATIVE (NPI) IS A GROUP OF individuals, some members of the NDP and some not, who believe that Canada needs a new progressive political party. We are calling upon the NDP, at its federal convention in November 2001, to initiate and support a process of outreach and consultation which would involve non-electoral social movements (such as the environmental, anti-globalization, labour, women's, anti-racist, gay lesbian and transgendered, anti-poverty, seniors, and disability rights campaigns); other left political organizations; and citizens' organizations (such as the Council of Canadians). This process would have as its goal the foundation of a new progressive party which would better unite the electoral and non-electoral constituencies on Canada's left, and which would highlight the central importance of democracy–struggling to protect and expand democracy in Canada, and practicing thorough participatory democracy in all its party structures.

WHO WE ARE NOT

Since the NPI website (www.newpolitics.ca) was first posted in early June, the media has paid a lot of attention to the NPI, not all of it flattering. Are we surprised? As a result, some of what NPI is trying to do has been distorted. Here are some corrections:

- The NPI is a call for a new party. The NPI is calling on the NDP to initiate and support a process of forming that new party. The NPI is not itself a new party.

- The NPI is about a new kind of politics. It is not a front for a leadership campaign. We have not even discussed the question of who should lead the new party we are proposing.

- Some of the founders of NPI are union activists and others are not. The NPI is not "union driven," whatever that means. We hope to have support from union leaders as well as social movement leaders. We believe strongly that the labour movement, along with other grass-roots social movements, should be integrally and organically linked to the new party. But this link must be built in a more authentic and democratic way than the current link between unions and the NDP.

- The NPI includes both those who are members of the NDP and those who are not. Some of our supporters believe that the NDP is capable of leading the process we propose and others are more skeptical. Nevertheless, we share the desire to see the NDP initiate and support the process of building the new party so that it can be built on the strengths of the old one.

- The NPI does not aim to divide the left. The left is already badly divided and that's part of our problem–divided between activists who work hard to build successful electoral machines, and those who work hard in extra-parliamentary campaigns for social change. These divisions come back to haunt us time and time again. We are aiming to reunite the electoral and social campaigning constituencies on Canada's left. We imagine a new progressive party that could both compete in elections, but also be more closely involved with the inspiring and creative energy of grass-roots campaigns.

WHAT WE PROPOSE

The core idea of the New Politics Initiative is simple, transparent, yet powerful. Public opinion polls continue to indicate that millions of Canadians have a deeply-held commitment to ideals of community, environmental sustainability, cooperation, equality, and public service. Meanwhile, grass-roots campaigns for social and economic justice, global solidarity, and environmental protection are getting stronger in the wake of failed right-wing pro-corporate policies. But the NDP, as currently constituted, no longer generates enough enthusiasm and support among these Canadians who hope and work most passionately for a better society, even though thousands of NDP members continue to participate actively in grass-roots campaigns for social justice, against globalization, and to protect the environment. We think that a new progressive political party–one which reintegrated the energy and commitment of the social movements with electoral campaigning, and one which put top priority on a new struggle for expanded democracy–would hold great potential for both strengthening the social movements and rebuilding a progressive electoral presence. So we have proposed that the NDP should initiate and support a process of outreach and negotiation that would lead to the formation of a new progressive political party in Canada.

HOW IT MIGHT HAPPEN

We are not asking members of the NDP to dissolve blindly the organization which they have worked so hard to build. We also recognize that a new party cannot simply be 'declared;' there must be an intense, participatory process through which the co-founding partners of that new party come together to realize their common potential and organize themselves in ways which celebrate their diversity of interests and methods but channel and unite their energies.

We imagine that the process of founding a new progressive party might look something like this.

Delegates to the federal NDP convention this November in Winnipeg would need to indicate that the NDP's best path to "renewal" lies in helping to found a new political party. The federal convention could then authorize the NDP's Federal Council to initiate a planning committee to enter into discussions on the formation of a new party. This process would need to be conducted in collaboration and cooperation with:

- leading organizations and activists in the environmental, anti-globalization, anti-poverty, labour, anti-racist, feminist, housing, seniors, gay lesbian and transgender, disability rights, immigrant rights, youth, urban reform, aboriginal, energy conservation, public transit, and other grass-roots campaigns and movements;
- other political formations including the Green Party, the Canadian Action Party, and the Rebuild the Left committees;
- and citizens' organizations such as the Council of Canadians.

The NDP cannot try to "own" or control this process. The NDP must enter this process honestly, as one of several essential co-founding constituencies. The vital and inspiring progressive activists who currently work outside of the NDP will have no confidence in a process which they see as merely an NDP effort to draw them back into the fold. They must be approached as equal partners in a creative and challenging process: trying to build an organization which reunites progressive electoral campaigning with the whole rainbow of extra-parliamentary social change activism.

If this process is successful in developing a concrete and broadly supported proposal for a new progressive political party, then the NDP Federal Council would authorize the NDP's participation in planning a founding convention for the new party. This founding convention would need to adopt a name and constitution, and elect a founding leader.

We imagine that this founding convention could be held by the end of 2003.

NDP members (like those of the other organizations and movements which must participate if we are to found successfully the new party) will naturally want to have a clear idea of what they are joining. For that reason, the NDP's participation in the formation of the new party would be subject to final ratification at a future NDP federal convention–either the regularly scheduled federal convention in fall 2003, or else an earlier special convention to be called at the discretion of the Federal Council. Contingent on that future ratification, the federal NDP would then become part of the new party as a founding partner.

THE NPI AND THE NDP RENEWAL PROCESS

The NPI actively participated in the NDP's official renewal process, meeting with the renewal Steering Committee, and presenting our views in numerous other renewal forums. Encouragingly, the first report of the official Steering Committee echoed many of the themes that have been stressed by the New Politics Initiative. The committee acknowledged that this is a time of opportunity and creativity on the left, not a time for retreat and concessions. But much or most of the new energy on Canada's left is found today outside of the NDP. The Steering Committee agreed that the NDP must reach out to those forces, and position itself more clearly and forcefully as a party of the left. The Committee even explicitly recognized the possibility of forming a new federal party as one avenue to revitalization.

Of course, one progressive-sounding report hardly constitutes the transformation of a party. Real challenges lie ahead in trying to convert the Steering Committee's recommendations into concrete changes in the NDP's policies and structures - rather than just another fine policy document which is subsequently ignored. It remains our view that the existing NDP will not credibly appeal to many of the progressive forces which have abandoned the party, unless and until more democratic and activist party structures emerge. We think that by agreeing to build, in genuine partnership with other left forces, a new progressive federal party, the NDP would send a clear and convincing signal to the broader left that it is committed to building a more effective and inclusive organization. The NPI will continue to work closely and cooperatively within the official renewal process (in addition to our other outreach efforts) to raise support for the concept of a new progressive party in Canada).

FEEDBACK

The NPI has received a lot of feedback from progressive Canadians, both positive and negative, on the idea of forming a new progressive party in Canada. In the spirit of the new politics we would like to see, we try to respond to this feedback openly. Our documents and our strategy have been changed and adjusted continuously in response to the concerns and suggestions that have been expressed.

NPI is too top-down, too Toronto-centred, too old, and not diverse enough:

We think the top-down criticism dissolves when people realize that we are a group of individuals simply trying to promote an idea: namely, that Canada needs a new progressive political party. We are not the group actually trying to start that party. We put up our web site as part of our effort to get broad grass-roots support for the idea of a new party from the beginning, rather than just contacting people we know across the country. This seemed the best way to kick start a more genuine grass-roots process.

About one thousand endorsers from across the country now formally support the initiative. We have set up regional organizing committees, and are hosting regional consultations (both large and small) to get important feedback and input on the idea of a new party, how it would differ from today's NDP, how it would work. The NPI itself is a work in progress, and we know that the project to build a new progressive party must becomes much larger than just the NPI. People from every region and every progressive constituency need to be involved in shaping and building that new organization.

The initial NPI Resolution was too much like an ultimatum to the NDP, and the party-building process was too fast to really develop a new party that is different:

We agree. In our enthusiasm we thought we could initiate a new party immediately after a positive vote at the November NDP convention. Clearly, this party-building process will take a lot more time, if we really want something broad-based and responsive to citizens at a grass roots level. So we developed a new sample resolution, which asks federal NDP delegates in November simply to approve the principle of a new party, and to initiate the party-building process. A subsequent NDP convention would need to approve the final outcome of that process. This approach also gives us more time to organize in support of this idea outside of the NDP and reach into diverse communities.

The NPI is too critical of the NDP. The NPI is a great idea but why tie it to a discredited NDP?

These contradictory comments, which we have heard time and time again, illustrate the problem that the NPI is trying to address. The divide between activists within the NDP and outside of it, in their perceptions of the NDP, is enormous. This has become even clearer since the NPI first issued the proposal to form a new progressive party. We are calling for a new party because the NDP in its present form may not be able to create the excitement and hope needed to reflect the new energy of the left in the electoral arena. But we are going to the NDP, asking its delegates to approve the idea of building a new party, because we recognize the NDP's long history and experience, as well as the thousands of wonderful activists within the NDP that the left needs.

I don't agree with this or that in the NPI's discussion papers, and anyway there's nothing there that the NDP couldn't support. Why form a new party for that?

The NPI is about finding new ways of doing *politics*, much more than simply developing new *policies*. We want to see a party that puts democracy at the centre of its concerns and actions. A new party should follow the principles of participatory democracy in its policies, its internal functioning, and its relationship to the community. We want to see a new relationship between that party, the labour movement, and the other social movements that have, up until now, seen themselves as non-partisan. We want to see a new party that is as active in the community as it is in Parliament.

Our initial "Vision Statement" mapped out this vision of a new, more movement-connected and democratic party. But it also contained some initial discussion of the sorts of policies we imagined that new party following: strong stands against globalization and environmental destruction, far-reaching measures to promote equality and participation in Canadian society, a willingness to start to name and challenge the power of private capital in our economy and our society. These initial ideas about the *policies* of the new party met with mixed reviews–and at any rate they were somewhat premature, in the sense that our priority is to build a more democratic and activist party structure, which can then develop its own policy statements as needed. So we downgraded that initial Vision Statement to a discussion paper, which has since been supplemented by other discussion papers on some of the crucial issues and challenges that will face a new party (such as how to more concretely define and implement the principle of participatory democracy; how to reconnect left politics with the bread-and-butter concerns of working people; and how to ensure that the face of the new left in Canada is no longer a white face, allowing us to build the new party among communities of colour).

We are confident that an authentic, democratic, and activist progressive party can successfully develop policies that will appeal to and motivate the grass-roots constituencies we need in our movement.

The main problem on Canada's left is not a lack of good progressive policy ideas–although we can always benefit from more creative and critical policy debates and discussions. The main problem, rather, is structural: the chasm that has emerged between the work of electorally-oriented parties and the day-to-day work of the activists and campaigners who are organizing for social change every day of the year. The NPI is focused on that structural issue. In particular, our goal is not to shift the NDP to the left: our goal is to build a more effective, democratic, and connected party that consequently becomes more successful in its efforts to convince *Canadians* to support more progressive policies.

A MOMENT OF OPPORTUNITY

Despite the social and economic victories of corporations and conservatives, vast numbers of people insist on continuing to fight for their basic rights to security, dignity, freedom, and environmental sustainability. They insist on continuing to make their own history, even as the spin doctors claim that history is over–that there are no longer any alternatives. These grass-roots struggles for a better world show no sign of letting up, despite the daunting power of the corporations and pro-corporate governments they confront.

We fundamentally reject the idea that the sun has somehow set on the ideals of egalitarianism, solidarity, redistribution, community responsibility, and socialism–ideals that have motivated generations of human beings to fight to limit the economic and political power of private wealth. If anything, as the incredible protests from Vancouver to Seattle to Quebec City have shown, *this is a time of opportunity for the left*. We celebrate the victories of our global movement: the defeat of the MAI, beating the pharmaceutical giants in South Africa, the strength of the Zapatistas, local victories around the world over water and waste, the rejection of neoliberalism in New Zealand.

The gap between the potential of our society to meet human needs and the grim reality we see around us every day is larger than ever. And wherever and whenever people are treated badly and unfairly, they find a myriad of ways to fight back and demand a better way. So long as this happens, the left has an important and influential role to play: speaking truth to power, challenging the right of the wealthy and powerful to oppress and exploit, demanding that our collective knowledge and talents be used to raise up human standards rather than enriching the few, mobilizing and inspiring people to fight for their rights.

Canada needs a forceful, ambitious, outspoken, and progressive political party, not only to contest elections, but also to fight more broadly for humane goals. We need a party that honestly challenges the assumptions and the outcomes of capitalism. We need a party that supports and links the day-to-day non-electoral struggles of Canadians for justice, equality, and sustainability, at home and around the world. We need a party which raises the expectations of average Canadians, who have been told from all sides that they daren't even hope for a better world.

THE FIRST TASK: BUILDING CANADIAN DEMOCRACY

The 2000 Canadian federal election should be a wake-up call to those concerned with the erosion of meaningful democracy at home and elsewhere. Voter participation reached an all-time low, especially among youth, as cynicism and mistrust of the political process reached an all-time high. Meanwhile, the corporations and wealthy who bankroll this increasingly expensive but shallow process were laughing all the way to the bank. It hardly mattered which business party won the election: huge tax cuts, delivering $100 billion or more to corporations and the well-off, were assured in any event. The election became a phony rubber stamp for decisions that were already made.

The left can and must reclaim the moral and political initiative in exposing this increasingly corrupt process, and demanding reforms which not only make our electoral process fairer–but more importantly put real decision-making power into the hands of Canadians every day of the year. We imagine that challenging the limits of Canadian democracy, and visioning and campaigning for the expansion of meaningful participatory democracy in all areas of our lives (not just at election time), can be a defining principle of a new progressive party.

Crucial changes must be made to our electoral system - and fast - to arrest the glaring decline in the quality of our elections and the quantity of citizens' participation. We must follow most of the rest of the world in implementing proportional representation structures. Campaign finance reform, barring corporate entities from using their money to manipulate and control our elections, is essential. Active enumeration programs must be reinstated, to reverse the alarming disenfranchisement of hundreds of thousands of Canadians–most of them poor. Teenagers today are clearly more educated and sophisticated than most adults were a century ago; all Canadians over 16 years of age should have the right to vote. We can push for structural changes to ensure that half of our parliamentarians are women.

But democracy means much more than just holding genuinely free and fair elections. There are infinite other ways in our society in which the ability to discuss and debate, to make decisions and control our own lives, is increasingly constrained and compromised. Our system of governance fosters a stratum of professional politicians and technocrats on one hand, and an inactive citizenry on the other; it promotes hierarchical and bureaucratic forms of government administration; above all, it tolerates and even promotes the concentration of private wealth and power which undermines the ability of Canadians to control their own lives on a day-to-day basis.

We demand a fundamental rethink of what democracy means to Canadians. Money and bureaucracy, not democracy, determines most of the important decisions in our lives. For too long social democrats have not seriously challenged this corrupt process, and hence leadership in the debate over democratic reforms has been ceded, ironically, to the right. Challenging this frightening trend, and recapturing the initiative in the struggle to defend and expand democracy, can be a crucial spark for revitalizing the whole left movement.

HOW SOCIAL CHANGE OCCURS

Just as democracy means much more than free and fair elections, so too does fighting effectively for social change involve much more than simply contesting those elections. We need an ambitious, principled party that participates in electoral contests. Elections provide a rare opportunity, in our generally depoliticized society, to discuss and debate crucial issues, and to present alternative visions before Canadians. And parties that win elections, of course, subsequently enjoy some ability to implement their policies and visions–although that ability is crucially constrained and tempered by the dominant economic power exercised in our society by corporations and the wealthy. As too many NDP provincial governments have found, you don't "win power" simply by "winning an election." Unless we are organizing and preparing ourselves to press actively for progressive change all the time, even winning elections may not advance our cause.

The most important task facing the broad left in Canada today is to nurture and build the myriad of campaigns and movements fighting for key improvements in society, the economy, and the environment, and to ensure that these movements have a strong and consistent political voice. To do this we need to expose simultaneously the growing failure of capitalism to meet our basic needs, but also raise hope among affected communities that better ways of doing things are possible. This will be a long-run, incremental process.

This central movement-building task is clearly complementary to the goal of electoral campaigning. When Canadians are motivated and mobilized, actively fighting for their rights every day of the year, they will be less apathetic and less subject to the shallow manipulation of electoral gimmicks. These movements can change the parameters of political debate. And they can win important

victories, between elections, even from business-oriented governments.

After all, that's how most important social programs in Canada
were implemented: not by well-meaning politicians who were
elected to bestow good deeds on a thankful populace from on high,
but rather thanks to passionate and engaged efforts by Canadians
to demand and win better policies and programs. Consider the
powerful victories that Canadians have won in recent decades–rang-
ing from improvements in women's legal and economic equality, to
better health and safety protections in workplaces, to the cultural
and legal liberation of gays and lesbians, to the development of a
deeply-rooted environmentalist consciousness in many segments of
society. These important victories did not come about solely or even
mostly due to benevolent actions by elected NDP governments.
What was crucial, rather, was a willingness by workers, women,
seniors, gays and lesbians, and environmentalists to stand up and
fight for their rights, for our rights. No matter who is in power,
building active and hopeful social movements–in a myriad of forms,
and using an infinite array of organizing techniques–is the crucial
prerequisite for further social progress.

Then, when election time comes, Canadians who participate
in these movements will naturally support candidates who have
won their trust in working year-round for their social and environmental goals. This requires that the demands of these movements
cannot be sacrificed in the interests of short-run electoral position-
ing by the political party; these demands, rather, must be front and
centre. And it means that progressive politicians need to be far more
forthright, energetic, and consistent than they have been in fighting
for these important demands, inside parliaments and out. When
left candidates are elected, they should become the parliamentary
voice of the active citizens' movements that are the real engine of
social change. Despite their current cynicism, social activists understand clearly that governments make important decisions and
that electoral processes are crucial to the evolution of society. They
can be won back to engaging again in electoral politics, but only by
a party that is seen to be an integral part of their struggles–not a
paternalistic elite that begrudges their independent capacities to
make demands.

This, then, is the core of the "new politics" that our initiative aims to promote. Politics is about the conditions of our day-to-day lives: how we live, how we work, how we relate to our environment, who has power, who makes decisions. Politics must change, and so must politicians. Our political leaders should see their main job as educating citizens about the failures of our system, motivating and organizing them to fight actively for redress–and then providing a parliamentary voice for the fightbacks we aim to inspire. Politics is not something we put on the back burner, until the time comes to gear up for another election. We don't want a "representative" politics, where we chose leaders to manage our concerns; we want a participatory politics, where our leaders march beside us in our common struggles (as NDP Members of Parliament did in Quebec City). Our goal is to empower and organize mass numbers of Canadians to fight for a better world–everyday, and everywhere. When we succeed in this, the left's electoral presence can only get stronger and more meaningful.

THE WAY FORWARD

The founders and supporters of the New Politics Initiative believe there is great potential in Canada to assemble a passionate, hopeful, and committed political constituency which rejects the cynicism of current electoral politics and the callousness of the market economy–a constituency which believes in the possibility of a better future. Thousands of young people in Canada are expressing their hopes and demands for a better future, in all kinds of ways: petitioning against sweatshops, riding their bicycles, organizing unions in retail stores and coffee shops, resisting racism and exploitation in their personal relationships, toppling fences at trade summits. At the same time, older generations of Canadians have maintained longstanding beliefs in goals of equality, security, and cooperation. This generational coming together of progressive values, combined with the failure of free-market capitalism to improve the life prospects of most of humanity or to protect the environment (whether in Canada or around the world), opens a unique opportunity for concerned Canadians to bring about great cultural and political progress. The apparent triumph of corporate capitalism rests on the assumption of continued popular acquiescence–and that assumption is looking more shaky all the time.

Many NDP members obviously share this vision of building a

democratic and mobilized social change movement. But the NDP as an institution can no longer claim to represent the enthusiasm, the vision, and the moral authority of many Canadians who long for fundamental changes in the way our society works.

We need a political party that concerned, progressive Canadians can support, without holding their noses, or needing to argue that it is the "lesser" evil. We need a political party that raises the hopes and expectations of Canadians demanding a better future, instead of explaining to them why their demands are not "reasonable" in light of modern realities. We need a political party which contests elections in an energetic and creative way–but which also understands the limitations of electoral politics, which fights for fundamental improvements in Canadian democracy, and which privileges the grass-roots activism of average Canadians as the crucial force in progressive social change.

The NDP has reached a historic juncture. It is time to reconstitute this party, time to build on its successes, but time to learn from its past mistakes. It is time to reach out to the legions of social change campaigners who presently see no future in conventional party politics, but also time to harness and reorient the energies of the solid committed people who still work within the NDP. Together we can build a force that will move mountains–re-inspiring a vision of a just and sustainable future, rejecting the selfishness and cynicism of the corporate-dominated model, and above all reaffirming the conviction that empowered communities can win great things for themselves.

---

* This chapter was collectively prepared and approved by the founding members of the national Coordinating Committee of the New Politics Initiative, including Morna Ballantyne, Murray Dobbin, Louise James, Dave Meslin, Judy Rebick, Svend Robinson and Jim Stanford.

The Truth Shall Make You Third

GERALD CAPLAN

APPARENTLY, IT'S 'BAD FORM' TO SAY THAT THE Canadian left can never form a national government. Either it's defeatist, or it gives the game away. I suppose both accusations are literally true. But it seems to me all but self-evident that the assertion itself is true. I'm far too old to harbour innocent beliefs that the truth will make you free. But what the truth can do, at least in this context, is to free us sufficiently to evolve a smart, realistic strategy that won't give us government, but will again give us some influence on the public agenda. That's always been the raison d'être of the CCF and NDP, and is to me an entirely satisfactory reason to carry on the struggle for equality and social justice. What's not good enough is neither to win power nor to have any influence. Alas, this has been the story of the federal party in the past decade.

Acknowledging the obvious may not even be a big deal. The evidence, after all, is not hidden away. There have been 20 general elections since the CCF was formed in 1932. At the very peak, in the eighties when Ed Broadbent was the most popular politician in Canada, we twice won 20% of the total vote. After the NDP replaced the CCF in 1961, we won 19% once, 18% twice, and 17% twice. That's it. Those were our peaks. That's when we counted, when we were THE third party, and occasionally people paid attention. WE were the only organized opposition to Trudeau's deplorable War Measures Act. We held the balance of power and used it to leverage important legislation.

In these same years, the NDP regularly formed provincial governments in BC, Manitoba and Saskatchewan, a circumstance generally reflected in the composition of our federal caucus after every election. Like the Alliance — in many ways, our mirror image from the right — we were overwhelmingly a western party, except that David Lewis and then Ed Broadbent hailed from southern Ontario and were very much central Canadians to their core. The two of them gave our western protest party a national feel. On the other hand, it was our bad luck that our votes didn't translate into seats in the highly efficient way that Reform/Alliance have done in three campaigns. (Although it must be acknowledged that we never came close to Alliance's 25% in1999).

Being led by central Canadians made the NDP feel more relevant to the national political scene. Beyond that, David and Ed seemed to matter to the larger world. They seemed personally to belong to the mainstream, in a way that Manning and Day never have. But the truth is that even at the pinnacle of our popularity, we were never real challengers for power. Today, having scored 8, 11, and 8.5 percent in the last three campaigns, we consider the achievement of simple official party status a great victory (well, a great relief, at least). We're almost wholly marginalized, and largely discredited in BC and Ontario. We have regressed to normal mediocre levels in Nova Scotia, we are precarious in Saskatchewan, popular only in Manitoba under a Doer government whose accomplishments are completely unknown beyond the province. It now seems a singularly ill-timed moment to pretend that a left government is anywhere in the offing in the lifetime of today's activists, or at least in the next couple of decades, whichever comes first. And thinking beyond 20 to 25 years is, surely, some other generation's planning horizon.

Of course there's Ontario. Whoever thought we'd win Ontario - ever! I for one did not. Isn't that the kind of defeatism that will become a self-fulfilling prophecy nationally? Well, no. In fact, it WAS unrealistic to think we'd win an election in Ontario. And the truth is, we never, ever ran a campaign as if we were going for government. In the legendary Lewis years, Party activists may have dreamed that the golden age was drawing nigh. But those who actually drew up the strategies had no such expectations—fantasies, maybe! When you were tossing in your bed in the middle of the night - Stephen and I have accused each other of such foolishness - we may have had fantasies, but never any serious expectations of the next breakthrough. That was the mood when we were routinely winning 26-28% of the provincial vote.

Nor was it different under Bob Rae. When Bob was agonizing over whether to leave federal politics and run for the Ontario leadership, he did not appreciate my flat assertion that he better not have delusions of grandeur. There was no chance, I warned, that he could beat history and political culture and take the Party to victory. He replied that he never did anything except to win. I assured him the Party's problem was a lot deeper than any one person. By his third campaign, he had come to understand what I meant.

To this moment, I stubbornly maintain that I was, in an important sense, right. Then the breakthrough came, in that miraculous, thrilling, unprecedented September 1990 election. WE had not won so much as THEY had lost. Our 1990 campaign was not aimed at victory; it was aimed at mere survival. I know: I wrote the strategy paper at a time when the Peterson Liberals were so far ahead that an election seemed almost a formality. As Rae has since admitted and as we all knew at the time, he fully expected to be whipped and to resign forthwith, his hopes dashed, my prediction sadly bore out.

Let me underline the key point. Even with 20% of the vote seemingly guaranteed, and close to 30% a realistic prospect, few serious people saw the Ontario NDP under Bob Rae as a contender. Some thought that by forcing Peterson to accept several important progressive policies in return for NDP support in a minority legislature, the party's credibility would soar. It was a reasonable gamble and it failed. The public thanked us by giving the Liberals a huge majority at the first possible opportunity. When Peterson took his own gamble by calling an early election three years later, he was unexpectedly punished. With Mike Harris, the new leader of the discredited third place Tories, peddling preposterous simple-minded nostrums, we were there to pick up the pieces. With 37.5% of the vote, we won a large majority. Go strategize and plan for a scenario like that!

However remote we are from power, I suppose nothing will ever stop New Democrats from introducing their leaders as the next Prime Minister or Premier. Since public polls demonstrate the dishonesty of these rhetorical flourishes, I've always hoped that voters would smile benignly at this harmless campaign extravagance rather than become indignant that their intelligence was being insulted in such a blatant way. Nor have I ever believed that our troops needed such BS to go out and work. NDP activists, in my experience, usually know the score, and if they're satisfied that their leaders are fighting a campaign of high purpose in an ethical way, if they're made to feel proud of their party, they'll enthusiastically respond in kind. People vote NDP because they believe in us, and because they know that the more NDP votes chalked up, the more influence we can have. And they'd be perfectly satisfied to have our leaders and candidates introduced accordingly.

We should acknowledge that our likely future electoral fate does not include forming the government of Canada. There are several reasons. First, it's demonstrably realistic. Second, it's telling the truth - a refreshing electoral innovation. Third, this insight would remind us of our indispensable historic role in Canada - to influence the public agenda. And that to do so we must have cogent policies and appealing ideas that we are able to communicate in the most compelling possible way. Des Morton once described that role as "a conveyor belt of ideas to the political system," an historic CCF/NDP function that was entirely usurped by Reform over the past decade. The great task in the next few years is to win back that role. Fourth, the obvious truth is that we have no idea how to change our electoral fate, because, if we did, we would have done so, long ago.. It's no act of cheerful masochism that's led several generations of Canadian socialists to find themselves not being the government of Canada. It's not as if they had the magic formula within reach and perversely chose to blow it because they loved being in opposition so much.

These fine folk have understood something which present critics within the NDP do not: if we move too far to the Left (whatever that means), we surely guarantee that those Party supporters who have defected to the Alliance or Liberals will forever shun us. And we thereby forfeit any likelihood that other parties might steal our ideas — our raison d'être. It simply baffles me how anyone can seriously argue that since Canada's only left wing party failed to get more than 20% support at any time in the its first seventy years of its history, becoming even more left wing will garner greater support in its second seventy years.

What exactly is the argument here? That all those trade unionists deserted us because we weren't uncompromisingly egalitarian enough about women's rights and minority rights and affirmative action, or because we failed to demand more public ownership, or because we failed to make more tax-and-spend promises?

If we move too far to the centre, however, we will find no room for ourselves, since the Liberals fill every inch of it completely. And if that's not enough for the Canadian public, so do the PCs. What baffles me about those who want the NDP to move to the centre is their illogical comparison of the Canadian with the European situation, above all in Britain. Through the entire time we've been the third (or fourth or fifth) party in Canada, Labour has been the government or official opposition in the UK. There is, in fact, no strategic or political parallel between us and Labour. Our plight is far more similar to that of Britain's Liberal Democrats, their third party. Moreover, Tony Blair is blessed, like his good friend Jean Chretien, with a self-destructive opposition, a far right and racist Tory party led by a man who makes Stockwell Day look attractive.

There are some simple rules to Canadian politics. Canada is characterized by having two more or less interchangeable mainstream parties that can be described as department store parties, or brokerage parties, or big tents. For a century and a quarter, these two institutions have evidently satisfied the political needs of a good majority of Canadian citizens. Few Canadian politicians have ever hogged the entire centre, from moderate progressive to moderate conservative, more skillfully than Jean Chretien, though I believe Paul Martin - a businessman who seems open and innovative - will succeed in precisely the same way.

But Canada has also had niche parties based either on region

(Bloc Quebecois), ideology (CCF/NDP), or a combination of the two (Reform/Alliance). For those hung up on the distinction, these can be defined as much as movements as parties. None of these niche parties has ever been able to attract more than a minority of supporters, nor have they been able to morph into bigger tents. Despite the apparent alienation of a growing number of Canadians with the existing parliamentary party system, and the present appeal of the progressive extra-parliamentary movement, I don't see any reasons to expect these historical patterns to shift dramatically.

I'm an historian by training. My first original piece of historical research was done just under forty years ago, shortly before the CCF was transformed into the NDP. The CCF at the time was lower than a snake's belly. We held government only in Saskatchewan, and had just been creamed in the 1958 Diefenbaker landslide. We barely counted on the political scene. Yet there were vague reminiscences from the Party's elders of a long-gone and all-but forgotten time when the CCF was a major political player in Canada. But there was precious little information on the subject. Recreating that period became the subject of my MA thesis.

From 1942 to 1945, I discovered, during World War Two - a mere twenty years earlier, remarkably enough - the CCF had come within four seats of winning the government of Ontario, very nearly won BC, did, of course, win in Saskatchewan, and on one historic occasion, in September 1943, actually led in a national Gallup Poll. In order to defeat this menace from the left, the mainstream parties reacted with a combination of vicious redbaiting on the one hand and, on the other, progressive policies that they had considered utterly anathema only a few years earlier. The entire tenor of Canadian politics changed in those few short years. The goalposts dramatically shifted to the left. Of course the bad guys succeeded in discrediting the CCF, and it never won a single government outside of Saskatchewan. But its influence was enormous. The postwar social contract that's so often spoken of was really forced on the political and business establishment at that time by the CCF's popularity and the growing strength of industrial trade unionism.

I consider Canada's modest welfare state to be among the country's most appealing virtues. This is a contribution to the public weal that can hardly be overestimated and it was in large part the legacy of a party that never formed a government.

My study also persuaded me that we who were advocating a socialist Canada were engaged in a Sisyphean task. The success of the redbaiting campaign against the party demonstrated the limits of the socialist appeal, and those limits were both clear and severe. Most Canadians didn't share the egalitarian, solidaristic, anti-corporate values espoused by the CCF. Canadians were not as narrowly individualistic or anti-collective as our American cousins. A modest amount of caring and sharing was okay. But on no account was this to be taken to the 'extremes' favoured by the CCF. These insights had been developed for the United States by historian Louis Hartz in the 1950s, and they seemed to me to usefully, if lugubriously, illuminate the Canadian experience. A few years later, Gad Horowitz enshrined them in his important essay "Conservatism, Liberalism and Socialism in Canada: An Interpretation." They seem to me largely true even now.

The popularity of left-wing values never again reached the levels reached during that war-time period. Nor did the left remain in that deep trough that characterized much of the 1950s. Once the NDP was created in 1961, it was able to woo enough votes or hold enough balances of power or exert enough moral influence to have other governments introduce progressive public policies from time to time. We counted! We helped set the political agenda. It was really only in the past 10 to 12 years that federal governments have felt able to ignore almost completely the arguments of the left and, on the contrary, felt the pressure to accommodate the dogmas of the right.

For a brief period after the Berlin Wall fell, some on the left dared to hope that the collapse of Soviet Communism might lead to a resurgence in support for democratic socialism. The anti-Communist card had long been used as an effective weapon against left-wing parties of all kinds. Now, it was hoped, the democratic left could position itself as the logical alternative to American-style capitalism. I was one of those who cherished this hope. As we know, the exact opposite happened. Market capitalism has been and remains triumphalist, everywhere! Think Tony Blair! *The Economist* supported Labour in the June 2001 elections as the embodiment of Thatcherism! Moderate conservatives have embraced formerly unthinkable positions, not least the need to reduce the role of governments in every area save enhancing the rights of the corporate sector. It has now become virtually impossible to run on a platform of higher taxes to pay for needed services (and Tony Blair assured *The Financial Times* that he won't raise taxes in his second term).

It's true that Canadians still give pollsters caring, sharing answers; many no doubt genuinely believe in a kinder, gentler Canada, and can't wait to pay more taxes in return for better services. That's become the self-image of many Canadians. They've been saying it for decades, and simultaneously voting 80%-90% for parties who offer the opposite. This was true even during the decades when Keynsian liberalism ruled the Canadian roost. Today, when 'neocons' have won the ideological day, when neoconservatism seems to be the natural and normal order of things, when absolutely every conviction of the left is on the defensive, those sweetly humane answers that pollsters record seem almost like a cruel joke.

Is this in any way controversial? Does anyone find that ours is a political climate in which social democratic values and policies are likely to be embraced, let alone one in which even tougher 'left wing' policies might be entertained seriously?

We on the democratic left have huge challenges to confront. It seems to me obvious that rather than self-deluding rhetoric about preparing for government, the first priority is rather more modest: simple survival. Then we must determine the values, policies and communication strategies that can return us to our former levels of support. We now have had three successive federal elections and many provincial setbacks to remind us that even these humble goals will be not be easy to reach. But if we fail, we'll be largely without influence, and we'll have lost our raison d'être completely. After almost seven decades of playing a remarkably positive and constructive role in saving this capitalist nation from its worst instincts, that would truly be a shame of immense historical magnitude.

Public Opinion and the NDP's Future: The Paradox in the Polls*

MARC ZWELLING

IF YOU ASK THEM, CUSTOMERS WILL TELL YOU HOW to make a profit, and voters will tell you how to win. On this assumption George Gallup launched the public opinion business more than half a century ago.

Should New Democrats fold the federal party or reinvent it? Should they forget about power – not just in the short term - but forever?

If the voters have given up on the federal NDP it doesn't matter what the Party does. It will die. But what do the voters say? There is no better way to find out than to ask.

If the Party is to renew itself its leaders must confront the truth: millions of voters like the NDP! The public wants the federal NDP to continue even if many New Democrats themselves aren't sure.

In May 2001, COMPAS Research asked a representative sample across the country whether the NDP should continue to run in federal elections or "find another role for itself."

• 29% said "definitely" run while another 19% said the party should "probably" run. Altogether half said keep going.

COMPAS also asked if voters agree or not with some reasons for voting for the NDP. Here is what the people say:

• 63% agree the NDP has a history of standing up for the poor.
• 57% agree the NDP stands for women's rights.

• 52% agree the NDP "backs high social spending by govern ment."

• 49% agree the Party wants high taxes on the rich.

• 48% agree it wants high taxes on corporations.

Seven months after the federal NDP's miserable outcome in the 2000 election, Vector Research + Development asked a representative national sample of eligible, voting-age Canadians how they would vote if a federal election were held now.

Vector also asked the voters who said they would vote for other parties, not the NDP, or who wouldn't vote or didn't know, to consider this scenario.

If you thought the NDP could win in the riding where you vote, how would you vote?

Here are the results of the two questions:

	NDP	PC	CA	LIB.	BQ	GREEN	OTHER
Initially	6%	17%	9%	55%	9%	1%	2%
If the NDP could win your riding	24%	15%	7%	44%	7%	1%	1%

Based on the 2000 federal election turnout every percentage point is worth nearly 130,000 votes. The NDP received an 8.5% share of the votes counted in 2000 (1,093,868). With the possibility of winning the voters' ridings the NDP captures another 2 million votes.

In this scenario, the Liberals, who won a third straight majority with 41% of the votes in 2000, would probably form a fourth majority government. The big change is that instead of considering its future the NDP would become the official opposition.[1]

What's the point of a pretend election if everyone knows the NDP can't win a real election?

No single poll or question proves the NDP can create a successful future. But many polls and opinion trends back up the scenario where the party captures 1 vote in 4.

Does the NDP really have so many silent supporters? The voters aren't lying. There is no reward for prevaricating to a pollster and no sanction for telling the truth.

In a memo to their patron, *The National Post*, COMPAS researchers Conrad Winn and Robert Laufer said, "If three out of every four voters who concede the NDP's mission ... actually cast a ballot for the NDP, the party would likely form a majority government." (*Post* editors didn't print this part of the memo in their news story on the poll.)

Why does half the country want the NDP around? Why are there so many more social democrats than New Democrats?

The federal NDP is not in trouble because voters have turned conservative or because social democratic values are out of style. The polls put the blame for the party's demise squarely where it belongs: on the NDP. Its candidates have failed to harvest their potential vote.

To reach its potential the party can start by courting its would-be supporters.

Elections tell us who won and lost. Polls tell us why. Like DNA, polls are unmistakable traces of voter sympathies.

For a free enterprise country Canada is remarkably ambivalent about the fundamentals of capitalism.

A fifth of the people wished they could be in Québec City for the anti-globalization marches during the 2001 heads-of-government summit on the proposed Free Trade Area of the Americas.[2]

Canadians are skeptical of the free trade cheerleaders.

• 49% don't trust what the federal government says on trade negotiations.

• 51% don't trust business leaders.

• 64% reject the business view that human rights and environmental considerations either don't belong in world trade deals or would be ineffective.

• 73% say Canada should not sign trade agreements that open domestic water systems to foreign ownership.

A true capitalist would leave the homeless and poor to the market and let the invisible hand meet their needs. But Canadians believe the tax system should redistribute wealth and equalize incomes. Voters tell opinion pollsters they would forego tax cuts or pay higher taxes to let government solve inequality.

In this social democratic-leaning electorate, how can the NDP fail?

Some in the NDP say the party needs to turn left while others say steer to the centre. In 21st century politics, however, the terms right and left are pointless and stand for anything you want them to mean.

Today's voters defy classification. EKOS Research Associates sampled Canadians before the 2000 federal election asking, "Would you say you are more small-l liberal or small-c conservative?"

A plurality – 43% - volunteered they were neither. The rest were 32%-22% liberal over conservative.

Advising the NDP to turn left gives the party no direction. Does it mean an overwrought business-bashing NDP campaign? That approach would exclude millions of potential voters. There are no more votes to be had for a party seen as anti-business.

Like it or not, the NDP's would-be voters work in that despised market. If going left means sulfurous anti-profit rhetoric it would marginalize the NDP even more.

• 41% of those who don't support the NDP say the reason is

that the party's policies are too extreme.

Others would not move left or right but wait for the political pendulum to swing. As the polls show, Canada has not shifted right, and so there is no right to swing back from.

Canada is hardly hostage to a right-wing agenda if you can get a prescription for marijuana and tan on a nude beach. Half would legalize marijuana (for personal use).

A 65% majority accepts gay and lesbian marriages. When nurses strike the public supports them.

76% would permit euthanasia. Entertainment and the arts are less censored and more uninhibited than ever. If Canada is moving right, what's it to the right of – Sodom and Gomorrah?

Voters are skeptical of giving business too much clout. Their expectations of business are out of sync with corporate performance.

- 82% say businesses sometimes should take smaller profits to meet their responsibility to their communities and workers. Just 18% believe corporations have only one responsibility "to make the most profit... even if this means reducing the number of people they employ."

Waiting to be swept to power is like awaiting the pendulum in medicine to bring back poultices and bleeding by leeches or expecting the technology pendulum to swing back to slide rules.

Even if there were a pendulum, waiting hands the Party's fate to others. Without a strategy, the NDP becomes part of its enemies' strategies.

There is plenty wrong in Canada. Poverty and inequality, however, do not prove Canadians are archconservatives or neo-liberals because the polls show the public supports government efforts to redistribute opportunity to the poor and disadvantaged.

There are signposts of class consciousness, too.

- Only 22% say people are poor because they don't try hard enough.

- 35% say people are poor "because the wealthy keep them that way."

New Democrats believe the country has gone to the right-wing dogs because most governments reduced their budget deficits in the 1990s. The public cheering for the deficit attack, however, was not about smothering the welfare state but about saving it.

To the people, deficits are a sign of government waste and inefficiency. If governments have unbalanced books the public fears precious social programs such as Medicare and Old Age Security are at risk.

Throughout the '90s people loathed deficits but continued supporting government spending on the problems that mattered.

> • By 66%-23% the public agreed in 1993 – while governments were hacking at deficits – that spending on infrastructure "creates good jobs" and is not "wasteful."

By 1995 people had had enough of cutbacks.

> • 56% said school classrooms were more crowded than five years earlier. Health care services were worse, said 54%.

> • A year later 62% agreed that "people are suffering because federal cutbacks have gone too far."

In his 1996 budget finance minister Paul Martin said he was "keeping on course." In the pre-election 1997 budget, the wind of public opinion at his back, Martin declared:

> "Having done what we had to do, we can see that the worst is behind us, that brighter days lie ahead… The era of cuts is over."

Nothing illuminates the Canadian political playing field as much as contrasting it to the American.

Which Canadian party leader could say …?

> *If we collect those taxes, government'll spend 'em. And we'll grow – at probably a faster rate than the economy does, and become an ever-larger percentage of our total economic activity in the country, and that'll be a mistake. So to some extent, by preventing government from collecting taxes that it currently has no use for, we avoid a situation in which we collect them and spend them and put them into the baseline to become a permanent part of the government."* — US Vice-President Dick Cheney[3]

The polls are consistent. More Canadians want to expand the welfare state than shrink it (just don't call it welfare).

> • Only 14% supported increased government spending on "welfare" in a 1996 poll, but 40% wanted more spent on "assistance for poor people."

Once the deficit struggles were over, the voters reprised their familiar role as supporters of state spending. A national Vector poll in 2000 asked, Do you agree or disagree –

> *Now that the federal government and most provinces have balanced their budgets and reduced or eliminated their deficits, there is enough money to expand Medicare to cover home care, long-term care, and prescription drugs without raising taxes or involving the private, for-profit sector."*

64% agreed.

Despite the turnaround in public attitudes toward cutbacks, support for the federal NDP continued to decline. The opinion polls prove the voters haven't rejected the NDP. The NDP has rejected the voters.

Those who want the party to have a future need to solve this paradox. Canadians are social democrats, but most don't support the NDP.

Is there a way to solve this contradiction?

The NDP has stumbled because it tries to sit two incompatible groups at the same table: politicians and utopians. As a result the party competes against itself.

The polls say those who scorn political power and believe the party should be a conscience, not a caucus, are wrong. A quarter of Canadians would vote for an NDP that could win.

One solution is to let the politicians have a political apparatus and spin off a subsidiary or affiliate for the utopians who want to take to the streets. Maybe call the non-parliamentary wing The Masses or Frontlash, or maybe the Woodsworth Corps or Battlecry.ca.

The extra-parliamentary affiliate would be in the streets

fanning the flames of discontent. The parliamentary NDP would be in the House of Commons preparing to replace the government. Some activists could serve in both the movement and the party.

Britain's Labour Party was a kind of political wing to the Fabian Society. Think of Greenpeace and the Green Party, whose memberships probably overlap (certainly their donors crisscross). In the US the National Rifle Association and the Republican Party could swap mailing lists or e-mail address books. But they have different missions.

The NDP was to be labour's political arm. However, only a minority of union members wants their unions to be a social movement or shock troops for a political party.

Why join a party or sit in its conventions if you aren't interested in political power? Those who eschew political power should seek power elsewhere… in art or music or business.

There is an ethical and possibly legal issue in accepting taxpayer-financed rebates for candidate expenditures and using the money for other purposes. Voters could complain to the regulators about misleading advertising.

Giving up on the federal NDP's chances patronizes the millions who would vote for it. It shows disdain for the provincial NDPs that have made it to government.

Tactically the federal and provincial parties might do each other a favour by taking different names. The reason most Canadians give for not voting for the federal party is the performance of the NDP provincial governments.

Cutting ties with the labour movement would not attract a lot of new federal votes because the labour link is not a big obstacle to people's voting NDP.

- 36% of non-NDP voters say they didn't vote for the party because "unions would have too much influence in an NDP government."

- But 4 in 10 say the party's provincial track record sours them on the federal NDP. In Ontario 6 in 10 say it's the provincial NDP's performance as the 1990-95 government.

Some ardent New Democrats frequently decry relying on the polls. The truth is the party has ignored public opinion. During the 2000 election campaign, the Party's exclusive focus on health care pretended political operatives can stir up issues. People, not parties, manufacture the issues.

Just as there is no right-centre-left spectrum, there is no single-issue bloc of votes. Health care was the most important issue – the issue that turned their vote – for only 25% of the voters. The NDP's addiction to health care wrote off the other 3 out of 4. Voters want to hear more than one tune.

At the end of the campaign single-issue health-care voters made up 41% of NDP supporters, a far higher percent than in other parties, which had more varied platforms and, not surprisingly, attracted more votes.

Even the way the NDP positioned health care defied opinion. To the public funding is not the only health care issue. A Léger Marketing poll found that a plurality, 36%, across the country say the health care system's problems are "mostly due to" bad management. Inadequate funding trails, at 31%.

Our values have shifted from a focus on what we have in common to what makes us unique. Voters want to know "what's in it for me?" The US Army caught this shift. Its new recruitment ads say, "I am an Army of one."

In the new political context a party needs an *assortment* of policies to have a hope of grabbing the voter's fleeting attention.

Voters have mastered TV. They can instantly decode a show's plot while channel surfing. Reaching media-savvy voters demands connecting with them viscerally.

To grow, the federal party needs to acknowledge what every voter knows. The kind of roguish capitalism NDP speechwriters defile has disappeared.

Canada is a social democratic country, maybe a social democratic oasis. Both public and private capital are legitimate to nearly every voter. The struggle is not between the public and private sectors, which have fought to a draw.

The struggle is to see how much of the public and private sectors' assets can be marshaled to save the planet from AIDS, global warming, malnourishment, crime, addiction, intolerance, water shortages, homelessness, poverty, and terrorism.

The NDP is staring at opportunity. There is little loyalty in the electorate. Between the 1993 and 1997 general elections half the voters switched parties. You attract these promiscuous voters with feasible, affordable, morally correct ideas that solve voters' problems. And because it's the age of televised politics you sell your ideas by keeping them short, simple, and specific.

For decades New Democrats have forfeited the market for ideas to conservatives. Canadians window-shopped and sampled some but bought hardly any. Voters are wary of privatization, business deregulation, school vouchers, and free trade.

They are also curious about them because New Democrats have given voters no alternatives. A bad idea sometimes beats a good idea, but a bad idea always beats no idea. The status quo is not an idea.

Manitoba New Democrats are the country's most successful NDP because they co-opt their competitors, the Conservatives, and have ideas of their own.

The NDP supported the Tories' law to make budget deficits illegal. The NDP won back the government in 1999 with 45% of the vote assailing the ruling Conservatives on health care but also on crime.

The government hiked funding to bring the Manitoba RCMP up to full complement for the first time in a decade. It has toughened measures against street gangs.

It passed a law requiring a referendum before Manitoba Hydro can be privatized. Its ministers contritely hand out small grants to corporations in the name of attracting investment, what used to be called industrial strategy.

The party liberalized the labour laws. It ended corporate and union donations to parties - an idea premier Gary Doer promoted twenty years earlier when he was a public service union president.

The government lowered hydro rates in rural and northern Manitoba to match Winnipeg's, creating one equal price throughout the province.

It expanded hours for private clubs, liquor and beer stores and let them open Sundays. "Manitoba's tourism industry will benefit from modernization of the Liquor Control Act," the minister for the liquor control commission explained. The NDP reduced and froze post-secondary tuition.

Doer notes among his achievements legislation closing loopholes "that would have allowed the proliferation of private, for-profit hospitals." And he enacted modest tax cuts.

Many New Democrats are wary of being a poll-driven party. When the NDP wins, however, it's because it listens to voters not because it defies public opinion. Since the voters are mainly social democrats, why not listen to them?

There are plenty of opportunities to campaign against deplorable business practices... routine discrimination against small shareholders... the pathetic amounts some businesses give to charities... inadequately tested products... bloated executive bonuses.

In all these controversies groups have organized themselves around corporate governance agendas. New Democrats can expand their vocabulary by catching the corporate governance movement to raise the party's visibility.

In Québec, where it has no roots, the NDP has been pushed aside by the Bloc Québécois and the Parti Québécois. In the rest of the country the opportunities are plentiful.

For a generation the federal NDP has defied public opinion and steadily lost voter confidence. Yet even at its nadir the party attracts the attention of 1 voter in 4. It's not hard or expensive to make the NDP a competitive party. But it's impossible if the party doesn't want to be one.

*A CAUTION TO READERS

My company, Vector Research + Development Inc., has never polled for the federal New Democratic Party or had any association with it. In early 2000 I was asked – among other firms – to bid on the party's election polling account. Another firm won the account. So my comments are hardly objective, but the arguments I make are supported by polls from my firm and several others with no links to the party. Therefore readers might study this chapter with special acuity in the way they would regard bidders who didn't get the Hindenburg job or the losing contractor who tendered on the Titanic. - *MZ*

---

[1] Given the margin of error for the COMPAS and Vector polls the 29% who say "definitely" run is equivalent to the 24% who would vote NDP if it could win the respondent's riding.

[2] Except as noted, all polls cited are from Vector Research national polls, 1997-2001.

[3] "Letter from Washington: The Quiet Man: Dick Cheney's discreet rise to unprecedented power," by Nicholas Lemann, *The New Yorker*, May, 7, 2001.

The NDP Is In Big Trouble. So?

CHRIS WATSON

THE NDP IS IN BIG TROUBLE AND EVERYBODY KNOWS IT. If we didn't know it in 1999 when we lost official party status in Ontario barely four years after having been in government, the Fall 2000 federal election made it hard to ignore. In that election better than nine out of ten voters across Canada cast their ballot for someone other than a candidate of the New Democratic Party. Then came the results of the British Columbia provincial election of 2001 - decimation, plain and simple. In Alberta, Quebec and three out of four Maritime provinces, we are almost non-existent, though that's nothing new and NDP'ers are used to it. In Manitoba and Saskatchewan where the NDP holds government, and in Nova Scotia where we are the official opposition, the Party looks healthy. But those three positive examples swim in a dismal sea, feeling now more like an accident then a natural outcome and we wonder about the future.

Since early 2001, the federal New Democratic Party has been officially engaged in a renewal process. All questions are on the table and some unofficial initiatives, such as the New Politics Initiative (NPI), have also come forth with proposals to remake the NDP into a new party. The NPI and some others argue for moving to the left. Others don't. Some want a new name. Others don't. But more and more people agree that the NDP, as it stands now, is in trouble and something needs to be done or it will continue a slide into relative political oblivion.

For some, the very best evidence that the NDP as Canada's political party of the left has become irrelevant is the degree to which the very noticeable and vibrant new mass movement against globalization ignore the Party. The throngs of (mostly young) activists going to Seattle, Windsor and Quebec City don't seem to hate the NDP. They just don't seem to think about it at all.

This movement, unparalleled since and reminiscent of the 1960's, has become something of a touchstone in the debate about the future of the Party, or whether it should have a future. It has become almost a given that an NDP (or something replacing it) worth its salt must be a Party that, at least, passes the litmus test of relevancy to this movement and those inside it.

For many it is obvious that the new and wildly successful anti-globalization movement contradicts anyone who says the left is dead. The obvious lesson would appear to be that if a party of the left would adopt a good portion of the views and methods and courage of this new movement, surely it too would be as vital. We could be celebrating victories instead of mourning defeats. There is a seductive reasoning at work here and the only way to assess it is to ask the question that, amazingly enough, is not being asked much inside the party or by those not actually in it but around it and engaged in the "where to from here" debate. The question? "Why is the NDP irrelevant to nine out of ten voters?"

THE REVENGE OF THE RIGHT

Starting around the time of the Thatcher/Reagan/Mulroney ascendancy, western industrial nations began to experience and continue to experience what might either be called the revenge of the right or a right wing cultural counter-revolution. The years between the end of the Second World War and the rise of Thatcher/Reagan/Mulroney were, in general terms largely experienced by the corporate elite and the established political right in the west as years of defeat. Defeat was perceived as an ever-broadening acceptance that our social-economic-political life was not best left entirely to the whims of the market and our corporate masters, but had to be protected by public institutions against the ravages of the market. Social equality/equity gained some measure of acceptance as a goal of society.

The success and institutionalization of the trade union movement, followed by the civil rights movement, the anti-Vietnam War movement, the rise of the women's movement, the peace movement, a powerful aboriginal rights movement in Canada and the United States, and emergence of the gay rights movement, the emergence of a powerful environmental movement, and the degree to which all these things reshaped both the popular political culture and values which became institutionalized in the laws and practices of governments in the West became the target for revenge by the right. Margaret Thatcher, Ronald Reagan, Brian Mulroney and more recently Preston Manning, Ralph Klein, Mike Harris and Stockwell Day became the figureheads of a powerful movement aimed at retaking power for those who took those earlier victories as defeats, who wanted to be restored to the throne and put an end to the "nonsense" that had become accepted wisdom.

It is worth remembering that it was not so long ago in political terms that women had to leave the country to get an abortion, we practiced the death penalty, and something as benign and commonplace as the Blue Box was no more than a silly hippie notion. It is only yesterday in historical terms that laws to protect gays and lesbians were unheard of. As were laws to force companies to recognize and bargain in good faith with workers through their trade unions and to sign legally binding contracts and to have to submit the resolution of grievances to binding third party arbitration.

By the 1990's, in Canada, there was a significant measure of institutionalized acceptance of anti-racism. We had laws against sexual harassment. We had laws banning the use of scabs. Birth control was not only legal, it was encouraged.

To people on the left all of these things represented small incremental gains in a much longer war. To the elites of the corporate right wing, these represented unbearable political defeats. They spurned an aching for the good old days and, not surprisingly, a thirst for revenge.

The right wing cultural/political counter-revolution has its most powerful political expression in Canada in the Reform/Alliance Party and Mike Harris's Common Sense Revolution each of which has had some success at redefining political values and retaking ground lost over previous decades. Don't forget that part of what inspired the Common Sense Revolution was the view that even the Progressive Conservative Party of Bill Davis had surrendered to left values.

Many people in Ontario experienced the Bob Rae/ NDP Government of 1990 to 1995 as, almost, status quo, as the establishment. But to a 1965 political mindset, it would have appeared as unbelievably revolutionary. And to people like Conrad Black, it did seem so. He even called on his class brethren to stop any new capital investments in Ontario until the NDP could be defeated.

Today, we in the NDP must remind ourselves that we have moved, quite quickly in terms of political history, into a world of new political values - a world where tax cuts are sacrosanct, a world where the idea of a government legislating employment equity requirements on the private sector, or raising welfare payments, as Ontario's NDP government did, seems incredible, a world where the new revelation was that the left's political solutions were tried and found failing.

In a few short and truly revolutionary (or counter-revolutionary) years the political question being asked was not even "should we go right or left?" but just "how far right?" Government and public institutions were discredited and identified as part of the problem not part of a democratic solution. The value of citizenship was demeaned and replaced by a celebration of individual self-interest.

The present reality is simple. Canadians have fallen prey to a new and very seductive argument; one for which the NDP and all of the left were entirely ill prepared. "Left political solutions have been tried and they don't work." After NDP governments in four provinces and a territory, after affirmative action and Medicare and public-this and equality-that we still have unemployment and poverty and we have discrimination and we have pollution and inflation and big shots who don't pay enough taxes and working people who pay lots of taxes and we have politicians who break promises and so on.

This shift redefined the political landscape in Canada overnight and although it might be argued that it has peaked, we certainly have not escaped its grip.

The other side of this coin is that many of the political values championed by popular movements have actually come to be seen as staid, or old hat, or yesterday's issue. The labels 'feminist,' or 'trade unionist,' or 'leftist' are not proudly worn on the sleeves of many young people today. Those who do wear them are old and middle class and do not look at all the like the wave of the future. After years of triumph, socialized medicine, and public education are now regarded as tired features of the status quo that might once have been great victories, but only in the minds of those old enough to remember. Today, it doesn't seem like blasphemy to question these things.

The political landscape has changed to the point where there are parties either ruling or poised to rule, who are farther to the right than anything experienced in Canada since the end of the second world war. The political centre has moved far to the right of where it languished for so many years.

NDP GOVERNMENTS — REMEMBERED AS DISAPPOINTMENTS

The belief that "left" political solutions don't work rests, in part, on the popular memory of NDP governments.

When voters ask themselves "what will we get if we elect the NDP?", the answer to that question is often the popular perception of the 1990-1995 Ontario NDP government. Rightly or wrongly that perception is one of disappointment, if not outright failure and even betrayal. The great irony is that we had raised such high expectations that even for those who have continued to vote for the NDP, there remains a bitter taste of disappointment. We asked people to expect more, and they did! The economy went 'stinko' and the popular perception was that we could not manage it.

In the cases of public auto insurance and the social contract, we were perceived to behave like the very politicians we said we would never be - the ones who would sacrifice any principle and make any compromise just to hold on to power.

The combination of a right wing cultural and political counter-revolution and a term in government by the NDP in Canada's wealthiest and most populated province that was experienced as a big disappointment if not a big failure, both dealt a body blow to the NDP and to the left throughout Canada. The party most wedded to government based solutions, to social and economic issues, had been given a chance and was seen to have failed. The apparent lesson was to turn away from collective solutions.

WE ACT LIKE WE DON'T DESERVE TO WIN

There is an old shibboleth that only in the NDP will some Party member call for a recount after we <u>win</u> an election. And it is not far from the truth to say that there are some in the NDP who see winning elections as problematic because governing requires compromise and makes you get your hands dirty and do things you'd rather not do. And there are those who, for less obvious reasons, have great difficulty going out on the hustings to tell voters that we are in this game to form a government and would make the best government of any party running.

A colleague of mine recently put it like this: "We have made it clear over the years and sometimes even state it during the election that WE ARE NOT RUNNING TO WIN. We are in the race for the Bronze medal; joined the pageant for the congeniality award; we want to do well but not too well; we have such confidence in our policies and positions we are asking you not to put us in control of the government; give us the keys to the car but we don't want to drive etc. etc."

To be blunt, there are days when it feels like we are trying to prove the old saying: "Act like a doormat and people will treat you like a doormat."

VOTERS CONCLUDE WE CAN'T WIN AND LOOK ELSEWHERE

In many cases, the most recent federal election being a good example, we go into an election in which it seems a certainty that we can't win and voters look for someone who can. This may be stating the obvious, but it has become even more so since the rise of extreme hard-right parties like the Alliance and the Harris Tories who turn voters into vulnerable and strategic voters.

The fact that some people, CAW Leader Buzz Hargrove being only the most visible, advocate strategic voting has only added to the perception that voters should be guided by something other than choosing the candidates or the parties that best represent their values.

All of this, of course, exacerbates that Catch-22 in which we can't win because we can't attract the calibre of candidates and the level of campaign money needed to win, and we can't attract those things because we are seen as unable to win.

These explanations - a cultural counter revolution by the right, NDP Governments seen as disappointments, NDP campaigns without the self confidence to say we should govern, and being labeled as losers - not only help us understand why the popular support of the Party lags so far behind what we believe is the popular value base, they also allow us to see the causes as being as much external as internal. They allow us to recognize the obstacles to be overcome.

WHY HASN'T THE NDP BEEN ON THE RADAR SCREEN FOR ANTI-GLOB ACTIVISTS?

There are probably many reasons why the NDP appears irrelevant to the Anti-Glob activists, not the least of which is that compared to participants of the anti-globalization movement, the NDP has grown quite long in the tooth. There is also the fact that the NDP tends to present itself as a parliamentary party and parliaments, I would think, are seen as part of the problem.

But the origin of the matter is more likely found in decisions made in the NDP in the late 1980's and early 90's with regard to the very issue of international trade agreements.

In the 1988 federal election campaign the NDP failed to make the fight against the looming Canada - US Free Trade Agreement the fight of its life and to stake its entire campaign upon it. As everyone knows, John Turner and the Liberal Party were not so squeamish. Perhaps thanks to their excessive experience at winning elections rather than losing them, they seized the issue, and became its champion.

It's not entirely clear why the NDP made that fateful decision. It is clear enough that the NDP has historically had a great complex about championing the same causes the Liberals do. And there certainly were stories in 1988 about how at least some high placed NDP'ers said "Free trade? Forget it - that's a Liberal issue."

Whatever the reason, the Party did not tie itself irrevocably to the only issue of the day, the fight against free trade. We lost inestimable numbers of votes from all those Canadians who did see it as *the* issue and who were more than ready to vote for Ed Broadbent. The Tories won, the deal was done and having made our bed we chose to sleep in it. International trade was not to be our defining issue. We were not going to try and rewrite history or refight lost battles. It was time to move on and we did.

In the years 2000 and 2001, those chickens have come home to roost.

We are living in a redefined political culture in which the argument "Left solutions don't work" has more purchase than it has for years. The popular recollection of our turns at power is one of disappointment. As a party we lack confidence in what we have to offer and, in most parts of Canada, we are branded as a party that just can't win. And for historically identifiable reasons, when young fervent citizens looked for political leadership on international trade issues, the NDP was not there.

The answer to our problem is not easy rhetoric such as "unite the left" or, for that matter, "move to the left," or "hold fast the course" or "give up the ghost."

THERE IS A SET OF CORE VALUES SHARED BY NDPERS AND BY MANY CANADIANS

Despite what election results might appear to tell us, there is a much bigger "we" than the NDP and its consistent vote may recognize. A large number of Canadians share a general set of political values. This value set was not created by the NDP and has been informed by much more than the NDP. But the NDP continues to be the only political party in Canada that, however ineptly, explicitly embraces it.

This value set includes the belief that big corporate power and their political friends continue to trash much of what is necessary to the good society, continue to cause or at least aggravate unnecessary suffering in the form of poverty and discrimination, continue to favour the wealthiest at the expense of the rest of society and perpetuates unnecessary damage to the natural environment. And that they are systematically dismantling institutions necessary to the kind of society in which we want to live.

These are the values that the CCF and the NDP have given voice to on the political stage. Despite what the naysayers would have us believe these values have not been abandoned.

Most of the people today debating the future of the NDP or the future of a left party in Canada, whether they are members of the NDP or not, also maintain an unshakeable conviction that the number of Canadians who still share our political values (loosely defined) far outnumber those who vote NDP.

There is evidence to support an assumption that many Canadians share the "core values" that hold the NDP together. Reams of issue-based polling data, and focus group results, and the doorstep discussions of literally thousands upon thousands of NDP campaign volunteers confirm this over and over again. It just translates less and less into Canadians' ballot decisions. We know that many who support what the NDP stands for, unfortunately do not vote NDP.

UNITE THE LEFT?

Social change in Canada requires political parties and social movements. Both have a different role to play. To play their roles they need to be independent of each other, free to articulate different views and to be critical of one another.

Social movements, in fact, are often in as much disagreement with themselves as with the NDP or anybody else. The last thing we should do is confuse the different roles played by a political party and by these movements by suggesting, as the New Politics Initiative does, that social movements should be brought into the Party (a new party) to determine the policy and practice of the Party in their given domain.

That being said, there is every reason to insist a successful NDP should be one that comes to enjoy the support of many of the activists in social movements and that the Party itself should be supporting those movements because they are fighting for the same things the Party is fighting for. And the NDP has a lot to learn from them in terms of taking a fresh look at what we are fighting for.

CONCLUSION

Yes, the NDP is in trouble. But, no, it is not because its basic positions and values are irrelevant. It is not because left political solutions don't work and it is not because it isn't "left enough", as anyone who has been to the doorstep for the NDP in an election campaign will tell you. It is also not because the NDP got lost on the road that led to Seattle and Quebec City. But it is equally true that we are staring straight into a mega vote-value gap. Many voters will voluntarily articulate much of the same ideas and values that we stand for, but they seem to live in a place where our language sounds old and dated, and where voters don't hear themselves when we speak.

The NDP should become obsessed with clarifying the vision of Canada that it wants to bring about. That, more than anything else, will attract, or not, the support of activists as individuals. If anything, that is what will allow voters to hear themselves when we speak, what will allow everyone to put the memories of past NDP governments into perspective, and set the stage for us to present, or re- present ourselves as a party with a vision of the future and a vision that we want to actually implement.

Once upon a time talking about Medicare, for example, put us far ahead of the pack. It was forward thinking. It allowed us to make real a different world, but yet a believable world, one that might really be brought about through political change. But we have gone so long since we have updated that vision that world has passed us by. Today even some of our best talk, like fighting to save Medicare, sounds like we are fighting to return to the good old days of the past. "Return to yesterday" just doesn't cut it in a political culture so steeped in small "L" liberal notions of progress and history.

Offering a vision of that world, a Canada in the year 2030, is an obligation of the Party just as much as it is the Party's obligation to work for the implementation of such a vision. If we are not ready to articulate a new vision of society, one that gives context to the struggles of others pointing in the same direction, and to commit to bringing that vision about, ultimately, though not exclusively, by forming governments, then we should get out of the business and leave it to someone who is ready to shoulder that role.

If we are in the political party business, then we have an obligation to tell Canadians what our society would look like in the year 2030. And if we don't tell them, they never will ask us. Arriving at a shared vision of Canada in 2030 from a social democratic perspective is the best way not only to move us beyond rhetorical debates, beyond less than stellar memories of NDP governments, beyond debates about unity without sufficient content as to what we might be uniting around.

Here is a first attempt at a 2030 vision, offered in the form of a news item.

THE ONTARIO DAILY NEWS DIGEST,
THURSDAY, JUNE 1, 2030

- The last of Ontario's Nuclear power stations was permanently closed today.
- The first graduating class of the Kapuskasing Medical School celebrated their twentieth reunion last night.
- The 2030 Commonwealth Games swim competition begins today in Hamilton Harbour.
- Ontarians go to the Polls today to elect 206 MPP's. Because of the province's Proportional Representation system pundits predict another minority government with as many as five parties represented in the House.
- According to the terms of Ontario's unique P.R. system, 103 MPPs will represent existing ridings while the other 103 will be selected from party lists according to the percentage of popular vote. Half the MPPs will be women.
- Special polling stations have been set up throughout Ontario's single secular public high school system, but predictions are that almost half the voters in the 16 - 19 age group will be voting on-line.
- University enrollment increased again this year. Undergraduate enrollment has risen steadily since the province implemented full publicly funded tuition for all university and community college students in 2009. Ontario now boasts the most highly educated population in North America.
- Muskoka University in Barrie led enrollment increases for the fifth year in a row reaching 10,000 full time undergraduate students.
- Since Ontario became officially bilingual in 2020, francophone student enrollment has doubled.
- Following the July 1st weekend all Ontario workplaces will conduct the annual Ministry of Labour supervised vote, allowing workers to opt for, or against, trade-union representation in all workplaces. The rate of unionization has decreased marginally since Ontario indexed the

minimum wage to inflation in 2010.

• Environmentalists will hold a celebration tonight outside the site of the former Ridge Landfill. The Ridge was shut down ten years ago today. Ontario first stopped licencing new landfill sites in 2009 after the NDP toppled the one term Liberal government.

• The Adams Mine Salmon Farm operated by the Algonquin First Nation celebrated its 20th year in business yesterday.

• Former Toronto Mayor Jack Layton Jr. announced today that he has accepted appointment by the provincial government for another 3 year term as CEO of Ontario Wind Farms Inc. Critics have complained that since Layton took over the operation six years ago, wind farm generation has held almost a virtual monopoly on new electricity generation in the province. Responding to critics, Layton said: "So, what's your point?"

• Ontario Premier Ramani Nadarjha said she was very pleased that Layton had accepted re-appointment and encouraged him to work cooperatively with the province's newer Ontario Solar Generation Inc.

• Thursday night traffic is lighter than usual this weekend. Ontario Northland Railway reports that since the opening of the third new line this year weekenders are leaving their cars at home and taking the train. "Ever since Ontario moved to the 4 day work week - our business has been booming," an ONR spokesperson said.

• A federal Report issued today says that Canada, once called a Climate Change Criminal for allowing the United States to set Canada's emissions policy, now leads the G8 in reducing Greenhouses gases. The report states that the reductions are due to strict pollution reduction measures instituted by the NDP Government in 2008 when the Government convened an Emergency Sitting in the House of Commons to deal with climate change. The unprecedented joint session of the reformed Senate, the newly expanded Commons and MPP's from all provinces and territories ran for 31 days without a break after the NDP Prime Minister announced the House would not rise until Canada had agreed to an emergency measures programme to curb climate change. The United States has refused to withdraw its formal protest with the World Bank asking for sanctions against Canada until the climate change programme is halted.

• Today marked the tenth anniversary of Canada's decision to forgive all outstanding debt owed to Canada by Third world nations.

Crafting the 2030 Vision is a task that needs to be started now, but it is not the only task. Just as the CCF concluded by the end of the 1950's that they had gone as far as they could and needed to remake themselves, in that case by uniting with Labour to form a new party, so to today is it time for a rebirth!

We took a risk in 1961 and we need to take a risk today. A big part of that could be by giving Canadians a reason to reconsider the profound cynicism they feel about politics and political parties by a commitment to new political forms. What could they be? Proportional Representation, and end to corporate and trade union financing of political parties, revamped election finance laws to counterbalance the undue weight that wealthy Canadians can assign to one party over another in an era when high priced television advertising is so determinant of election outcomes, moving to one member one vote for selecting the party leader.

The NDP in Canada has too much to offer and its roots are too deep to be thrown away, but at the same time, it has too little bankable political currency to continue with just a little tinkering.

The NDP is in big trouble. So? So, lets look at why and then do something about it. The truth is the time is ripe. The rhetoric of the right is growing stale as it finds itself more and more at odds with the reality in which Canadians live. In politics nothing lasts forever and the seduction of the hard right has past its peak. NDPers across Canada have taken their heads out of the sand, and this is a grand beginning and no small accomplishment. Let's take a deep breath, roll up our sleeves and get to it.

THREE:

WHAT'S LEFT?
Public Policy and the New Democratic Party

Do Canadians care less – on know less? Learning from the high-civic literacy Scandinavian welfare states

HENRY MILNER

SOCIAL DEMOCRATS ARE WEAKER POLITICALLY IN Canada than in pretty much any comparable country. Yet Canadians are hardly less caring – and in many cases more caring - than people in many of them. For example, the 1992 ISSP Survey showed Canadians to be closer to Swedes than Americans in their views about whether the government has a responsibility to reduce income disparity. And, indeed, in that survey of 11 industrial democracies - including Sweden – Canadians were the least likely to agree that income differences are needed for the country's prosperity (Pammett and Frizzell, 1996: 174, 176).

So what's the explanation for Canadians' failure to take that concern to the ballot box, and what, if anything, can be done about it? It would be comforting to think that if the NDP changes its program and its leaders the voters will flock back. I suggest, rather, that the problem is deeper, that it has something to do with the institutions and policies affecting what Canadians – as opposed to people in European countries where Social Democrats are well entrenched – know about politics and public affairs. It begins from the simple fact that not only do a lot of Canadians not vote NDP, a large and increasing number don't vote at all.

In the November 2000 federal election, for example, fewer than 60 percent of potential voters made it to the polls. Part of the problem is that young people are increasingly turned off party politics, a problem affecting the sources of support for social democratic parties in a number of countries, and one addressed elsewhere in this volume. But there's another aspect that is seldom addressed. When turnout declines, the groups that are most affected are usually those on the margins, with low economic and educational resources,[1] those lacking the basic information to use their vote effectively. Yet these are the people social democrats seek to address and whose support they require.[2] And, where social democracy is strong, this is just what continues to happen.

While we have not quite reached American levels, levels of political information in Canada are low and in decline.[3] And here, I contend, lies the root of the problem. In the summer of 2000, the final report of the International Adult Literacy Survey (OECD, 2000) was released. (The IALS test assesses the extent to which people in 20 countries possess the ability to read the texts needed to function as an effective citizen.) In it appeared a particularly striking chart, reproduced here as Figure 1, that dramatizes the close relationship between income equality (as measured by Gini coefficients[4]) and functional literacy.[5] Its message is dramatically clear: *democratic societies that more equally distribute intellectual resources also more equally distribute material resources.*

How does this happen? The answer, I suggest, emerges from another chart using the same IALS data, this time combined with from data that I have assembled[6] for voter turnout averages in local elections. Figure 2 shows that *democratic societies that more equally distribute intellectual resources attain higher levels of civic engagement.* Combined, the message from these two charts is that because they promote higher levels of political participation, societies that more equally distribute intellectual resources, i.e., high-civic literacy societies will also be those that, over the long term, more effectively redistribute material resources. This is a fundamental, though neglected, element of the Scandinavian social democratic welfare state. Since informed individuals can better identify the policy options of different parties and thus their effect upon their own

FIGURE 1.

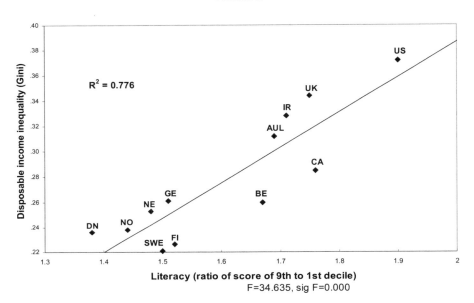

Literacy (ratio of score of 9th to 1st decile)
F=34.635, sig F=0.000

interests and those of others, high civic-literacy societies are more likely to attain relatively egalitarian social outcomes. Conversely, because those excluded through lack of civic competence from informed participation tend to be those at the bottom of the social ladder, the cost of low civic literacy is borne especially by the economically disadvantaged.

Below I describe some of the ways Scandinavian and Northern European countries achieve high civic literacy and thus attain the level of informed political participation needed to support social democratic policies. While I am persuaded that implementing such policies could and, in the end, would strengthen the position of the NDP and social democratic politics and policies in Canada, this is not the point I wish to stress. For one thing, this is not the kind of reasoning likely to persuade those currently in a position to implement these policies. Rather, I argue for policies to enhance civic literacy as a good in and of themselves, a means of preserving the achievements of a socially just society in which a great many Canadians who do not vote NDP take pride. Most of my examples are drawn from Sweden, the country I know best after Canada.

FIGURE 2.

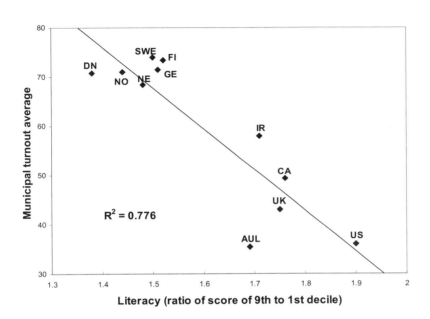

STUDY CIRCLES AND ADULT EDUCATION

Civic literacy is central to Scandinavian social democracy. For example, the official position paper on EU membership of the Swedish Social Democratic Party (SAP) begins by proclaiming: "that everybody is both desirous and capable of playing a part in the running of society... of acquiring knowledge and insights which will enable him to play a part in the life of the community" (SAP, 1993: 6). Readers are invited to consult my earlier work (Milner 1989; 1994) which describes how the policies and institutions of Scandinavian welfare states, sometimes known as the "Swedish Model," directly and indirectly foster a more informed population which uses that knowledge, in turn, to reinforce more egalitarian outcomes and institutions.

My work was much influenced by one of the fathers of the Swedish Model, trade-union economist Gösta Rehn. One of Gösta Rehn's main concerns was to help labour leaders explain the facts and analyses underlying the policy positions associated with the applications of the Rehn-Meidner economic policy model[7] in a manner understandable to the rank and file and consistent with their experience. Indeed, application of the model was premised on a high level of civic literacy, that is, on the expectation that people have the sophisticated historical, geographical and economic knowledge to place their own choices as workers and citizens in the context of their wider and long-term interests. The premise was based especially on the efforts of the ABF, the Workers' Educational Association. The ABF, which is affiliated with the main trade union confederation, LO, and the SAP, long ago committed itself "to educate the members of its affiliated organizations for positions in associations, working life and society; and to create conditions for everyone to participate in freely chosen education and cultural life."

Today, the ABF annually organizes about 100,000 study circles for over a million participants. It is the largest of 11 adult education associations organizing study circles and related activities. As reported by a Royal Commission in 1998, there were 336,000 study circles in 1997, lasting an average of 35 to 40 hours, with a total of over 2,844,000 participants for a population of under 9 million. For example, the fall 1999 program of the ABF in Umeå (where I was teaching) offered the usual range of courses in languages, computers, art, music, and nature appreciation, but also courses in organizing groups and co-operatives, in public speaking, writing and understanding media, as well as study circles on social and civil rights, the United Nations, war and peace, the future of democracy, feminism, various aspects of history, and important contemporary books.

Such courses supplement more specific courses given by the trade unions themselves to enable members to improve organizational skills, interpret financial documents, and understand economic and social policies. Local trade unions also appoint "book ombudsmen." In addition, adult education societies in that year organized 165,000 miscellaneous popular cultural events (a number that has been rising steadily), as well as 38,000 non-course pedagogical activities, such as conferences and lectures.[8]

A comparison with Canada is found in a rare comparative study of adult education. Table 1 shows that not only do Canadians - as expected - participate less in adult education than Swedes, but that the difference is especially acute among those with less formal education.

PROPORTION OF PARTICIPANTS IN ADULT EDUCATION (1983)

Educational background	Canada	Sweden
Fewer than 9 years of schooling	5	21
Upper secondary school	19	46
University education	45	64

TABLE 1. *Source*: Rubensson,1994.

THE MEDIA

Even more important in enhancing civic literacy than adult education are policies that reduce dependence on commercial electronic media by promoting newspaper reading and the development and use of non-commercial electronic sources of public-affairs knowledge. Norway, Finland and Sweden[9] subsidize daily newspapers that are not leaders in their markets (Sanchez-Tabernero, 1993: 229).[10] The subsidies traditionally account for 3 to 4 percent of all newspaper revenues (Hadenius and Weibull, 1999; Salokangas: 1999).[11] There is an unambiguous relationship between such government efforts at encouraging newspaper reading and national circulation figures, as a glance at Table 2 bears out. Scandinavia stands out as that corner of world where reading daily newspapers remains an unquestioned part of everyday life.[12] Over 80 percent[13] of people over 16 read at least one reasonably good daily newspaper, with little variation by gender or even educational background (Hadenius and Weibull, 1999: 149).

Related to such measures are concerted efforts to encourage the reading of books, through both subsidies to publishing and distribution, and programs offered by local public libraries. Libraries in Sweden, for example, provide free home delivery for shut-ins and services to hospitals and homes for the elderly. And a special newspaper, *8 Sidor,* containing national and international news articles written in easy Swedish for those with learning difficulties or new to the Swedish language, is widely distributed. Another exemplary measure is the program that places in the hand of the district public-health nurse at the time of the first post-natal home visit "The Child's First Book," a compilation of rhymes and stories for children, to underscore that reading, like proper nutrition and hygiene, is vital to the development of a healthy child.

On the electronic side, despite the recent inroads of commercial broadcasting, it is still fair to say that in all four Nordic countries public-service channels remain dominant, if not always in audience share, certainly in setting the standard for news and public affairs. The proportion of Swedes watching at least one of the public television news broadcasts has remained steady, even among young people.[14]

One other policy with a very pronounced positive effect on reading bears mentioning: all foreign language television programs as well as films and videos are subtitled. This is due to the fact that the populations speaking the Nordic languages are small, making dubbing very expensive; but it is also a matter of a conscious policy choice to promote reading. Given the number of dubbed films and – though less so - TV shows they watch, Quebeckers would especially benefit from such a policy.

ENHANCING TRANSPARENCY

Newspaper subsidies were established not simply to foster diversity in the media, but also to facilitate the political parties publicly presenting their views.[15] Conversely, but for the same civic-literacy related reason, the Scandinavian countries are among the strictest when it comes to equal access to television. Sweden and Norway have, by and large, eliminated political party television commercials. Overall, written information remains a significant feature of Nordic party politics.[16] So do study circles: each of the Swedish parties is associated with one of the adult educational associations, which, especially during election years, arrange study circles to familiarize members and sympathizers with party programs and strategies.[17]

Civic literacy is also enhanced by regulations governing the availability and accessibility of information related to the public interest. There are two key guarantees related to civic literacy: first, the requirement that tax-return information be public,[18] and, second, the obligation of all public institutions to open their books to interested citizens, with ombudspersons appointed to ensure that this is done (Axberger, 1996).[19] Moreover, high civic literacy is manifested in the relative absence of a "digital divide." By the beginning of 1999, 60 percent of Swedes responded positively when asked if they used a PC in their own home, twice the European average, while 40 percent had a home connection to the Internet, compared to a European average of only 8.3 percent. Swedes also led in interest in, and willingness to pay for, on line/interactive training (Eurobarometer #51).[20]

CIVIC LITERACY AND CONTINENTAL INTEGRATION

Related to civic literacy is the Scandinavians' attitude toward Europe. On one side, they display "Europeaness" in their openness toward people from other European countries, fluency in European

Country	Daily Newspapers per 100 population*
Austria	40
Australia	26
Belgium	31
Canada	22
Denmark	33
Finland	52
France	21
Germany (W)	33
Ireland	19
Italy	11
Japan	58
Netherlands	30
New Zealand	30
Norway	61
Sweden	51
Switzerland	39
United Kingdom	38
United States	24

TABLE 2. *Source*: UNDP: 1997: 204

languages, and propensity, when young, to travel and live outside their national boundaries.[21] Yet they evince a high level of awareness of the possible dangers presented by continental integration to the institutions that have secured egalitarian welfare outcomes. Norway remains outside the EU; Denmark and Sweden are members, but, unlike Finland, have eschewed monetary union.[22] All three members all strongly insist on transparent relations with the EU[23] and oppose political union into a federal Europe.[24]

POLITICAL INSTITUTIONS

From the perspective of the analysis offered here, a federal Europe threatens the Scandinavian welfare state primarily through its effect on civic literacy. To remain informed, citizens need a comprehensible political map. In a federal Europe, such a map must not only set out the relationship between the institutions of their own state and those of the supranational bodies, which is complex enough, but also the cultural-ideological-institutional context in which representatives from other member states to a directly-elected European parliament/government operate. Only elites are in a position to make effective use of such a map, not the mass of people whose primary interests lie in the reinforcement of the welfare state.

Canadians could stand to learn from Scandinavian attitudes toward European integration in coming to deal with the institutions of North American economic integration. But the clearest institutional lesson to be drawn from the social-democratic welfare states concerns the electoral system. Many NDPers have, only now, faced with the possible extinction of their party under our first-past-the-post (FPTP) system, come to appreciate the benefits of proportional representation (PR). But fairness to small national parties is only one of the advantages PR would bring. As I argue in detail elsewhere (Milner 1999), the well-established turnout boost associated with PR is, in large part, an expression of civic literacy. Since every vote counts under PR, each voter in a PR election is like a resident in a highly contested single-member district.[25] But civic literacy is the key: it is less a matter of the individual's increased chance of affecting the outcome, which, in reality, is still minuscule, than of the different incentives placed on political parties.

These incentives affect, firstly, how parties invest their limited resources. In a first-past-the-post election, parties ignore many voters, concentrating effort and money on voters in close contests.[26] Unlike PR, FPTP exaggerates a party's geographic weak spots, creating a disincentive against involvement in regions where it has relatively little support. Under PR, in contrast, parties have an incentive to inform all voters of their programs.

They also have less of an incentive to conceal or dilute their defining principles. The representational logic of PR-based, multi-party systems is to inhibit precipitous changes to a party's principles and identity, that is, the elements that constitute its place on the political map. Political actors, and the voters themselves, can thus count on a clearly drawn and stable political map on which to plot their own paths. For political actors, this includes reliable expectations about which other actors to cooperate with and over what issues. Under FPTP, on the other hand, electoral prospects are maximized by targeting the median voter, leading to the blurring of genuine policy differences between major parties and an undue emphasis on personality and exaggerated rhetoric at the expense of policy debate. Policy differences are replaced by distortions and exaggerations, since FPTP-based political actors have an interest in misrepresenting the policies of other parties in ways likely to cause them electoral harm. Under PR there is less incentive for political leaders - who may very well need their opponents' support to form coalitions after the election - to inhibit the awareness of the electorate of alternative positions on the issues of the day.

The absence of PR thus means a public less politically informed than would otherwise be the case. And, by making it easier to identify with a political party, PR fosters political participation especially at the lower end of the income and education ladders where information is at a premium. It is no accident that the most egalitarian countries use PR while the increasingly inegalitarian English-speaking countries are those still holding on to FPTP.

CONCLUSION

We can now put flesh on the relationships starkly portrayed in Figures 1 and 2 on which we began. Those who wish to preserve and improve that which makes Canada relatively egalitarian should push for policies to make it easier for Canadians to be informed citizens. Policies must foster newspaper readership, discourage commercial television watching, promote continuing education.

Priority must be placed on changing the electoral system and related aspects of political institutions affecting civic literacy. In the long run, the higher civic literacy attained through such reforms will make it easier for social democratic defenders of the welfare state to win support and attain office – and use office to reinforce these policies. The long-term goal is the kind of virtuous circle attained in Scandinavia: an informed population supports (social-democratic) policies that result in egalitarian outputs and outcomes and reinforce civic literacy thus enhancing political participation.

If such choices are not made, we face a vicious circle: declining civic literacy, a further decline in political participation, - especially among those at the margins - and mounting economic inequality.

REFERENCES

Axberger, H-G (1996). "Public Access to Official Documents." *Current Sweden* #414. Stockholm: Swedish Institute.

Bennett, Stephen E. et al. (1995)."The Impact of Mass Media Exposure on Citizens' Knowledge of Foreign Affairs: A Five Nation Study." Presented at the Annual Meeting of the American Political Science Association, Chicago, August 1995.

Daniels, Norman, Bruce Kennedy, and Ichiro Kawachi (2000). "Justice is Good for our Health," *Boston Review* 25, 1: 4-10.

Government of Finland (1996). "Finland's Points of Departure and Objectives at the 1996 Intergovernmental Conference." Report to the Parliament by the Council of State, 27.2.1996.

Government of Sweden (1996). "The EU Intergovernmental Conference 1996." Government Report to the Parliament, 1995/96.

Hadenius, Stig and Lennart Weibull (1999). "The Swedish Newspaper System in the Late 1990s. Tradition and Transition." *Nordicom Review*, 1999, 1.

Hoest, Sigurd (1991). "The Norwegian Newspaper System, Structure and Development," in H. Roenning and K. Knulby (eds.) *Media and Communication*. Oslo: ISAF.

Howe, Paul (2001). "The Sources of Campaign Intemperance," *Policy Options,* January-February 2001.

Kangas, O and V-M and Ritakallio (1995). "Different Methods, Different

Results: Approaches to Multi-dimensional Poverty." Presented at the ISA Research Committee 19 Conference on Comparative Research on Welfare State Reforms. Pavia, Italy, April, 1995.

Leighley, Jan and Nagler, Jonathan (2000). "Socioeconomic Class Bias in Turnout: Evidence from Aggregate Data." Presented at the American Political Science Association's annual Meeting: Washington, September 2000.

Milner, Henry (2001). *Civic Literacy: How Informed Citizens Make Democracy Work* Hanover N.H: University Press of New England.

— — — — (2001a). "Civic Literacy in Comparative Context: Why Canadians Should be Concerned." *Choices*. Montreal: IRPP.

— — — — (ed.) (1999). *Making Every Vote Count: Reappraising Canada's Electoral System*. Peterborough: Broadview.

— — — - *(1994). Social Democracy and Rational Choice: The Scandinavian Experience and Beyond.* London: Routledge.

— — — — (1989). *Sweden: Social Democracy in Practice.* Oxford: Oxford University Press.

— — — — and Eskil Wadensjö (eds.) 2001. *Gösta Rehn and the Swedish Model at Home and Abroad.* London: Ashgate, 2000.

OECD (2000). *Literacy in the Information Age: Final Report of the International Adult Literacy Survey*. Paris: OECD.

OECD (1997). *Literacy Skills for the Knowledge Society: Further Results from the International Adult Literacy Survey*. Paris: OECD.

Pammett, John H. and Frizell, Alan, eds. (1996). *Social Inequality in Canada*. Ottawa: Carleton University Press.

Rubensson, Kjell (1994). "Adult Education Policy in Sweden, 1967-1991" *Policy Studies Review*, 13, 3-4: 367-390.

Salokangas, Raimo (1999). "From Political to National, Regional and Local. The Newspaper Structure in Finland." *Nordicom Review*, 1999, 1.

Sanchez-Tabernero, A. (1993). *Media Concentration in Europe*. Manchester: European Institute for the Media.

SAP (1993). "Social Democracy on the Eve of the EC Membership Negotiations." Official translation of position adopted by the Parliamentary Group, January 19, 1993.

Søllinge, Jette (1999). "Danish Newspapers. Structure and Developments." *Nordicom Review*, 1999, 1.

UNDP - United Nations Development Program (1997). *Human Development Report*. New York: Oxford

Worre, Torben "European Integration, Legitimacy and Democratic Representation: Danish Perspectives." Presented at the ECPR Joint Session of Workshops, April, 1994, Madrid, Spain.

---

[1] This has been especially well documented in the United States. A recent American study found that: "the voting rate of persons below the poverty line was 25% in 1992... and of persons above the poverty line ... was 65% (Leighley and Nagler, 2000:1).

[2] Even after adjusting for other factors that might predict state welfare policy ... robust relationships were found between the extent of political participation by lower-class voters and the generosity of state welfare payments in American states. In other words, who participates matters for political outcomes, and the resulting policies have an important impact on the opportunities for the poor to lead a health life (Daniels et al., 2000: 9).

[3] In the 1984 Canadian Election Study, close to 90 per cent of respondents could identify their provincial premier; this statistic fell below 70 per cent in 1997. Between 1990 and 2000, the proportion of Canadians who could not name the Prime Minister went from 5 to 11 percent (Howe, 2001). An international study of political knowledge, conducted in 1994 by the Times-Mirror Center for the People and the Press, asked representative samples of the population in five countries five questions about international affairs. Canadian respondents (at 1.9 average correct answers) placed above the Americans (1.7 right answers), but below the British and French (both 2.1); German respondents (at 3.6) were far and away the most knowledgeable (Bennett et. al, 1995: 43). A study of first-year university students, reported in the spring 1995 *Bulletin* of the Canadian Political Science Association found the British to score 50 percent higher on questions about past and present political leaders, and 75 percent higher in ranking foreign countries on the basis of population and GDP than both their Canadian and American counterparts. For more detailed information see a paper by the author recently published by the IRPP (Milner 2001a).

[4] The possible minimum Gini is 0.0, i.e. all income equally distributed; the possible maximum is 1.0, i.e. all income going to the 10 percent of households receiving the most income.

[5] This chart is derived from that published in the final report (OECD 2000). The chart plots the ratio between the score at the 10 percent level and the 90 percent level in IALS results in each country.

[6] See Chapter 3 in Milner 2001

[7] According to the model, which dominated Swedish policy making in the 1950s and 60s, active labour market policies would move trained workers from declining to expanding industries, promoting optimal labour-market

choices on the part of workers and consumers (well-informed through the network of adult-education oriented activities noted above). Moreover, non-inflationary growth could be attained by enlisting the support of labour as well as employers for tight fiscal and monetary policies to enhance the demand for, and supply of, appropriately trained workers - their mobility underpinned by universalistic welfare-state guarantees. A detailed discussion of Rehn's contribution is to be found in Milner and Wadensjö (2001).

[8] Moreover, adult education neither begins nor ends with the study circles but extends to the municipally-run *Komvux* courses for completing compulsory and upper secondary education, the various programs offered annually to some 200,000 Swedish adults in the 140 Folk high schools, and the labour-market training courses run in close collaboration with employers' organizations and trade unions.

[9] The only other country known to this writer with direct subsidy programs is Austria.

[10] These benefit to an amount between 5 and 35 percent (averaging around 11 percent) of revenues.

[11] Not surprisingly, among European countries, Norway, Sweden and Finland rank first, second and fourth in daily newspaper titles (Sanchez-Tabernero, 1993:40). In 1990 there were roughly 275 daily newspapers in the three countries plus Denmark (Hoest, 1991), which have a combined population slightly lower than that of Canada - where, by way of comparison, there were 106 dailies in 1995.

[12] A survey asking Finns to identify the essentials of life that state welfare programs had to meet found that 55.3 percent of respondents regarded a daily paper as a necessity of life, a proportion placing it above 25 of 37 consumption items including television, stereo, video, cinema and new clothes (Kangas and Ritakallio, 1995: Table 1).

[13] In Denmark (in 1993), 78 percent of men and 71 percent of women read daily newspapers. Denmark has never directly subsidized newspapers (Søllinge, 1999).

[14] This information comes from personal communications from Bengt Nordström, who is responsible for monitoring audience magnitude for SVT. A recent study conducted at Göteberg University shows further that even with the increase in private station viewership, the feared "race to the bottom" has not materialized

[15] While not as partisan as they used to be, Scandinavian newspapers generally still identify with a party.

[16] One manifestation is to be found in the political information kiosks set up during campaigns. The visitor to a Swedish city or town square will encounter wooden huts reminiscent of the summer cottage (*stuga*) where parties distribute their programs and campaign literature and where candidates and party leaders meet electors.

[17] The discussion of political issues need not be partisan. Special study circles are organized to consider vital issues of the day. Over 50,000 people participated in ABF study circles on EU membership in the period preceding the 1994 referendum. An even greater number participated in the latter half of 1995 in response to a report by a all-party parliamentary commission looking into changes in the structure of European institutions (that became the Amsterdam Treaty).

[18] The principle is that paying taxes is a public and not a private act. All aspects of personal life are sheltered from public view; but tax revenues make social services possible. Hence keeping its sources secret would contribute to public ignorance over policy alternatives and arouse suspicions that others' are not paying their share. The public thus knows, for example, how much of the King's income goes toward taxes. When journalists write about public (or even not so public) figures, they usually include annual income in the profile (along with age, marital status....)

[19] The facts and figures on spending by governments and public institutions, and the results of comprehensive and detailed research into the effects of that expenditure, are widely disseminated. The result is that you don't need an accounting degree and the resources of an investigative reporter to understand public finance.

[20] The same proved to be the case in response to a question about interest and willingness to pay for access to electronic information on products such as videos, music, CD's, books, computer software or hardware.

[21] *Eurobarometer* #51 (p. B12) found 31 percent of both Swedish and Danish respondents to be "very attached" to Europe (second only to the Luxembourgeois).

[22] When asked whether they identified with their nation or with the EU in *Eurobarometer* #50 in the fall of 1998, the Swedes were second highest (60 percent compared to 62 for Britain), followed fairly closely by the Danes and Finns (with 53 and 52 percent) to identify exclusive with their country.

[23] Real democratization, the Scandinavian members insist, is really a matter of public access to EU operations and documentation. For the Danes, it was only when transparency in European Council activities was guaranteed that they were willing to reconsider the Maastricht treaty they had previously rejected by referendum. Sweden waited only three months after entering the EU to join in the Danish-led push for removing the veil of secrecy from EU institutions. The Finns took a similar position, stressing access to documents. Both new entrants insisted that this aspect of transparency be included in the EU treaty.

[24] A solid majority of Danes continues to insist that "member states retain full sovereignty and the right of veto" (Worre, 1994: 2). And in their official statements to the EU Intergovernmental Commission which drafted the Amsterdam declaration, the two new Nordic EU members made their position clear: "The Finnish government's ... point of departure is that the

Union's character as an association of states should be preserved" (Government of Finland, 1996: 24). "The Swedish government's starting point is that the EU would continue to develop a community of independent states to which some decision-making power may be transferred, so that common goals may be more easily achieved" (Government of Sweden, 1996: 13).

[25] We know such districts experience higher turnout. For example, the Center for Voting and Democracy's statistical analysis of the 1994 elections for the US House of Representatives reports a clear correlation between margin of victory and voter participation, with a 13 percent difference in turnout between the 87 most contested and 54 most lopsided districts.

[26] Concerning the November 2000 US election, "the National Journal ... reports that ... four of the nation's top eight media markets — Boston, Dallas, New York City, and Washington, DC — had a grand total of six presidential ads aired, while eight media markets in battleground states each aired more than 6,500 presidential ads." (November 22, 2000, electronic report of the Center for Voting and Democracy, accessed via www.fairvote.org.)

New Economic Radicalism:
Ten small steps towards democratic socialism

PIERRE DUCASSE*

DEMOCRATIC SOCIALISM IS NOT MERELY, OR EVEN
essentially, a question of quality social programs; neither is it merely
a question of redistribution of wealth. Democratic socialism is more
than just a means to mitigate the negative effects of capitalism. As
social democrats, we have been guilty of indulging in reductionist
discourse for far too long. It is now time to look towards the future.

SOME PRELIMINARY CONSIDERATIONS
I wish to propose a vision of the future for our movement.
This vision, which I would describe as economic radicalism, is
founded on several principles:

1) Our discourse, that of the democratic left, must focus on economic
issues and at the same time demonstrate how and under what conditions economic development can be compatible with social development and justice.

2) We must define our purpose in terms of challenging the capitalist system and working continually towards democratic socialism, which is characterized by: community ownership of a majority of means of production, economic democracy, public and community control of investment, full employment, a fair and social market-place, and sustainable development. However, we should not aim to overturn capitalism overnight; nor should we simply attempt to humanize it. We should aim to build an alternative, slowly, yet surely. This is what Michael Harrington calls visionary gradualism.

3) In order to achieve our goals, we must proceed with a certain prudence and great patience. The society we dream of will not come to exist within a year, 10 years or even 25 years. Nonetheless, we must continue to move forward, keeping our focus on the future. This means we must propose well-thought-out, practical, realistic measures that are not merely likely but certain to find favour with the public. Our individual policies must target dealing with the consequences of social and economic problems and at the same time strike at their underlying causes.

4) To implement the measures required to challenge the very foundations of capitalism, social democrats must gain control of the reins of government power. Contrary to some social democrats' beliefs, we will never achieve the adoption and implementation of these measures while sitting in opposition. Nevertheless, before forming a majority government, we must, of course, succeed in setting a new political agenda, one that is quite different from the current one. This is precisely what I call, in this particular context, radicalism.

CONCRETE STEPS TOWARDS DEMOCRATIC SOCIALISM

The policies we implement must play a double role. First, in the short term, they must counter the harmful effects of the current economic system: they must bring about immediate and appreciable improvement in the quality of life of all citizens, especially the most disadvantaged. Second, in the long term, these policies must attack the very foundations of the wealth-amassing capitalist system. This should not require two distinct groups of policies; rather each measure should simultaneously aim to meet both objectives.

The following is a list, although not exhaustive, of measures that are consistent with these goals:

1) WORK-SHARING

Contrary to what some politicians would have us believe, unemployment remains a serious problem in Canada. Official figures are grossly undervalued, excluding hundreds of thousands of people, notably welfare recipients who are fit to work. We are also witnessing an alarming trend whereby a growth in economic production is no longer necessarily accompanied by a corresponding increase in employment. The consequent technological advances and increased productivity lead to the elimination of a large number of jobs in both the production and service sectors. Moreover, a large upswing in the number of workers with part-time or temporary status has been observed: we must therefore be concerned about inequalities within the working class itself.

In light of this, I believe that the reduction and sharing of work hours is fundamental to a new strategy for full employment. Since work is not merely a commodity but an element of human dignity, full employment and reducing disparities between workers (permanent and temporary, full-time and part-time) are issues that are as much ethical as economic in nature. True social justice therefore requires not only the sharing of wealth by a society but the sharing of the means of producing this wealth, notably work. We should proceed gradually however, beginning with incentives to employers, workers and unions. A Canadian work-sharing policy should go hand-in-hand with other measures, measures dealing specifically with distribution of purchasing power and training. Our goal must always remain clear: creating and maintaining jobs while reducing socio-economic inequality.

Full employment under fair conditions brings us one step closer to democratic socialism.

2) LOCAL INVESTMENT

Capitalist globalization, by imposing free circulation of capital and investment, reduces the ability of states and communities to control their own principal economic levers. The current economic system encourages an excessive concentration of ownership of capital and means of production. In addition, there is a lack of capital devoted to alternative projects at the local level. For example, resource regions need to develop new undertakings in the area of secondary processing. Also, projects in the area of co-operatives or social economy have only limited access to venture capital. Similarly, we note that a large part of the capital held in retirement funds by Canadians is invested abroad, constituting a significant flight of capital. Rather than courting foreign investors on bent knee, the Canadian government should attempt to mobilize Canadians' savings inside Canada.

We should therefore turn to alternatives that encourage local investment and development. To this end, we envision the establishment of Co-operative Local Investment Funds. The mission of these locally owned and controlled Funds would be to act as levers of development. They would invest mainly in SMEs, co-operatives and social economy enterprises and could be finaced by three different methods: 1) contributions of individuals in the form of RRSPs under the same favourable conditions as Labour Funds; 2) a significant transfer of moneys from a special tax (of perhaps 2%) on capital gains; and 3) direct contributions from local companies. This would constitute a new method of redistribution, moving from a private capitalist system towards a co-operative, community-based system. The State would thus be the driving force behind this redistribution but would not benefit from it directly: democratic socialism does not equal statism. Local development and local investment would be the watch-words of a renewed socialism.

Community-based capitalism under local control brings us yet another step closer to democratic socialism.

3) SOCIAL ACCOUNTABILITY OF COMPANIES

Neo-liberal ideology tends to deny companies' social responsibility. Nevertheless, any economic activity has an impact, or external effects, which goes beyond the balance sheet and the relationship between producers and consumers. We do not currently posses any commonly recognized instrument to evaluate companies' impact, good or bad, on society.

Any company, whether private, public or co-operative in nature, should be required by the Canadian government to provide a social audit. To do this, clear indicators of social profit and loss would have to be developed. These indicators could be developed based on the following 10 considerations: 1) type of ownership and distribution of profits; 2) openness and accountability to the public; 3) creating and maintaining jobs; 4) work conditions and labour relations; 5) participation of workers in decision-making and co-management; 6) relationships with partners; 7) environmental impact; 8) contribution to the community; 9) impact on quality of life; and 10) respect for internationally recognized human rights. A rating could be given for each of these factors. A social balance sheet, verified by an external body and accessible to the public, would have advantages for consumers, investors, communities and the state, as well as for socially responsible companies. The government could take measures, incentives at the initial stage, to motivate companies to improve their score (for example, by making a good social balance sheet a condition of any government subsidy). The implementation of a social audit should not simply aim to force a good conscience on companies; on the contrary, it should be used as a tool to counter current practices and thereby render companies more responsible. This would create a favourable environment for the development of other models in the long term.

Open and responsible capitalism brings us yet another step closer to democratic socialism.

4) CO-OPERATIVES AND SOCIAL ECONOMICS

Social democracy has long been strongly linked to the idea of a mixed economy. The neo-liberal steamroller tends to impose a single model: private enterprise. Conversely, social democrats tend to look too often for solutions inside the state. Social democrats should not depend solely nor mainly on the state but on the dynamic sources of civil society. Private enterprise, the state and the co-operative/community sector are the three components of a real mixed economy.

The federal government should introduce various mechanisms to support the development of enterprises in the community sector. A ministry for the development of co-operatives and social economy enterprises should be introduced to: 1) manage an Investment Fund in the co-operative and community sector, using loans at low interest rates; 2) co-ordinate support programs for co-operatives in other ministries. There is no reason why the co-operative model could not be applied-or reapplied-to a number of fields of economic activity (agriculture, insurance, distribution networks, housing, transport, recreation, etc.) A new generation of co-operatives, modeled on Québec's coopératives de solidarité, could emerge. It would be a simple matter to set clear objectives such as, for example, doubling the number of co-operatives operating in Canada within 10 years. In addition, a significant contribution could be made by Co-operative Local Investment Funds, which would invest at least 25% of their capital in co-operatives or social economy enterprises.

Co-operative capitalism brings us yet another step closer to democratic socialism.

5) DEMOCRATIZATION OF THE WORKPLACE

The alienation of workers with respect to production methods has not vanished with the decline of industrial society; it simply exists in new forms. Stress and lack of motivation in the face of daily work are indicative of this. In fact, democracy is not often seen in the workplace, which tends instead to be ruled by feudal principles. Yet we spend most of our lives in the workplace and not in the voting booth on election day.

Democratic socialism is not merely a question of redistribution of wealth but a question of citizens' democratic control over the means of production. Incentives could be created to establish sectoral programs encouraging industrial democracy and worker involvement in decision-making and profit-sharing. Pilot projects could be set up to encourage the creation of new models of community ownership and democratization of the workplace. Within 10 years, it is hoped that the number of enterprises taking this road would triple. To achieve this goal, we must not only encourage unionization but also work towards building a renewed labour movement. It should be noted however that these measures, which should be accompanied by appropriate training, do not represent an end in and of themselves; rather they are a means of allowing workers more control of their own enterprises.

Capitalism accompanied by participative democracy in the workplace is another step towards democratic socialism.

6) ECOLOGICALLY SOUND DEVELOPMENT

As we all know, environmental protection is becoming an

increasingly important policy matter in today's world. The current discourse of many ecologists contributes to supporting the idea that protecting the environment and economic development are somehow incompatible. We must change our thinking on this issue, but there is some good news and some bad news. The bad news is that there is an urgent need for us to change our consumption patterns and production methods. The good news is that this challenge could be translated into a significant economic generator. The time to think of ecologically sound development is right now.

A new Green Technology Investment Fund could be set up to encourage research and investment in new production methods (cleaner production processes, treatment of waste, new sources of energy, electric transport, etc.) Taxing gas by only 2¢ per litre could generate a Fund of more than $4.5 billion within five years. This Fund could be used to create jobs, especially in research and implementation of new production methods.

Sustainable, ecologically sound capitalism brings us another step towards democratic socialism.

7) DEBT REDUCTION

The federal deficit is now under control, but the debt of the Canadian state is still very high. The debt burden has the tangible effect of transferring money from the poorest taxpayers to the upper middle class, the rich and bankers. Interest paid on the debt represents 23% of federal expenditures, a large sum that in the short- and medium-term is not invested in other public services (health, education, infrastructure). Servicing the debt constitutes 5% of the GDP, and foreign debt is at about 10%.

Debt reduction should not be a cause championed only by the right. On the contrary, we not only should, but must, bring a leftist perspective to this issue. We must make debt reduction a priority, but in a way that is consistent with the principles of democratic socialism. Specifically, we must re-examine the role of the Bank of Canada and ensure domestic financing of the collective debt. We must also oblige various deductible RRSP investment funds to hold a higher percentage of Canada Savings Bonds. Co-operative Community Investment Funds would also be expected to put at least 30% of their capital into Canada Savings Bonds. This would mean that financing the debt would no longer be a burden but a means of financing local investment. Moreover, with a policy of low interest rates, we could establish clear objectives with regard to lowering the debt/GDP ratio within 10 years..

Reducing our dependence on financial capitalism brings us another step closer to democratic socialism.

8) REDUCTION OF PERSONAL DEBT

Private and household debt has reached alarming proportions in Canada. In the year 2000, 75,000 people declared personal bankruptcy. This is not surprising since the consumer debt index is near 23%, not including other debt. (Neither is it surprising then that the average savings rate fluctuates between 2-3%.) This phenomenon actually represents a transfer of wealth from middle-class families to their bankers. This is unacceptable: it is totally counter-productive in the long term for a society to tolerate such a transfer of money from the real economy to the paper economy.

We must make reducing private debt, especially consumer debt, a priority. We should start with campaigns to educate people about debt overload and overconsumption. Furthermore, the financial system must be more closely regulated, particularly where credit cards are concerned. Maximum interest rates should be set for all cards (8% higher than the Bank of Canada's key interest rate for example). Measures should also be taken to reduce access to credit. This would liberate significant sums to families who could then choose to spend or save more. Pawnbrokers should also be subject to extremely strict regulation. Finally, in addition to the preceding measures, we could encourage the creation of community lending circles.

More exchange in the real economy rather than the paper economy brings us closer to democratic socialism.

9) A UNIVERSAL ALLOCATION

Traditional socio-democratic discourse maintains loudly and clearly that the goals of economic viability and social equity are not mutually exclusive. This is clearly true; however, we cannot fall back on this position to justify the status quo in terms of social policies. The social safety net that was built over the past forty years has now reached its limits: current welfare programs have proven to fail in achieving their principal goal, to lead people out of poverty.

Current programs create a strong dependence on the State, stigmatize their recipients, invade people's private lives, and are extremely regressive in their application. We must cease to think in terms of such a social safety net, which benefits only the poorest in society and instead think in terms of a social springboard, which benefits everyone.

A universal allocation is simple, efficient and just: it is income that is granted uniformly to every citizen from the cradle to the grave. In the long run, this measure would facilitate the elimination of a large number of current programs that target a specific clientele. These programs are counter-productive and serve only to maintain an army of civil servants overseeing overly complex programs. The advantages of a universal allocation would be numerous: improving the lot of disadvantaged workers; easing the transition period between jobs, training, unemployment and vacation; increasing the overall stability and predictability of income; avoiding the exclusion of people from specific programs; creating strong incentives to work. A universal allocation should go hand-in-hand with a truly progressive taxation system. It would also be a powerful tool in promoting social solidarity by alleviating tension between "taxpayers" and recipients of government programs. This universal allowance could be implemented gradually over a 10-year period.

An egalitarian and unconditional revenue security program brings us closer to democratic socialism.

10) NEW INSTITUTIONS FOR GLOBAL ECONOMIC CONTROL

Capitalism has established itself as being increasingly global. But globalization does not only affect capital; it also poses incredible challenges in the renewal of socio-democratic thought. Should we be content to simply reaffirm our "sovereignty" and attempt a return to a national economic system of a Keynesian type? Not necessarily.

We should instead establish Canada as a world leader in creating new institutions and mechanisms for global regulation. We should follow the example of the Lisbon Group, which calls for the adoption of new world contracts on social justice, the environment, culture and democracy. In this context, the hypothesis of a world government seems inevitable. However, the construction of this alternative, socio-democratic globalization, would not be accomplished in a few years. This is a project for the next fifty years, which is why it is important to start yesterday. New global mechanisms of economic regulation should be created: minimum union standards; international equalization; investment in infrastructure and social development; international anti-monopoly and anti-oligopoly laws; taxes on financial transactions. Should we start thinking in terms of a world-wide Keynesian model? I believe that the Canadian government can play a leadership role in this area.

A better-regulated global capitalism, for the common good, brings us yet another step closer to democratic socialism.

CONCLUSION

The democratic socialism of the future must take a new stand with respect to the marketplace and the state. Our task is not to discredit the state but to rethink it. Our task is not to take a stand for or against a market economy but to know which type of market economy we want. The alternative to a free capitalist market is not a powerful State; it is rather a sustainable, community-based, democratic and co-operative marketplace. The role of the state must change within this context: it must not only concentrate on government social programs and the means of economic regulation but must also concentrate on initiatives directed towards changing the very structure of our current economic system.

Two objections could easily be raised to the "ten steps" outlined in the preceding pages: first, that they already exist within western socio-democratic parties, one of which is the NDP; second, that the proposed measures are moderate in the end and do not deserve to be called radical. Regarding the first objection, I would say that some of these ideas can be found in existing political programs in written form, but that they are still not part of the political discourse of any party leader in the public forum. For example, during the federal election campaign in 2000, NDP discourse concentrated almost solely on health care and not on the most important economic issues. Regarding the second objection, what is important is not specific measures but their long-term objectives and impact. We should have enough imagination to see the structural changes that could result from an ensemble of measures that in and of themselves may appear to be moderate.

We must move from a socially democratic welfare state towards a state that is socialist in its policies. We must work towards solving social and economic problems as well as challenging the system that caused them. I believe that this approach is not only electorally marketable but could serve to reconcile different trends within the New Democratic Party. Concentrating on economic issues and adopting a strategy of pragmatic radicalism is a winning formula for Canada's left.

*The author wishes to thank the following people for their assistance: Philippe Bélanger, Steve High, Brenda Plant, JJ, Clément Laberge, Tom Vouloumanos and Peter Graefe. Thank you to Kelly Ann Sullivan for the French-English translation.

A New Perspective on Health Policy for Social Democrats

SHOLOM GLOUBERMAN

THE CANADIAN MEDICARE SYSTEM HAS BEEN AN important part of Canadian federalism for more than thirty years. For a long time Canadians were among the most satisfied people in the world with how they received health care. By the late 1980s, this began to change. Health care inflation and fears about the sustainability of current health care systems resulted in a process of retrenchment and restructuring. By 1992, growing public concern and dissatisfaction led Michael Decter to observe that Canadians were no longer smug about medicare.

Things have not improved. We remain worried about the current state and future prospects of medicare. There are a number of widely acknowledged problems. Public confidence has eroded to the extent that many Canadians are not sure that the system will be there should they need it. Overcrowded emergency rooms, intolerable waiting lists, crises in cancer care and even in the water supply, fuel this anxiety. Health care professionals are dissatisfied with the current state. They feel overworked, underpaid and seriously un-dervalued for the services they provide.

Recent increases in funding to the system have momentarily reduced public anxiety but it is widely believed that this is only a short respite. Most significantly there are apparent threats to the guiding principals and values that lie behind the system. Some would argue that all five principles of the Canada Health Act are threatened today, in one way or another.

• The Canada Health Act guarantees Canadians coverage for medically necessary care in hospitals or by doctors. As pres-sures reduce the scope of what is considered medically neces-sary, what is medically possible has expanded. This disparity creates tensions around the public's understanding of com-prehensive care. Hospital stays are shorter and people are sent home earlier and are required to care for themselves after their stay in hospital. Some services have been "delisted" to save money for the system Recently, for example, physiotherapy outside hospitals, which is not under a doctor's supervision, was delisted in Ontario. This means that less physiotherapy will be available because it is unlikely that hospitals will in-crease the amount of physiotherapy they offer on an outpa-tient basis. At the same time people expect more from the healthcare system. As more and more conditions, from in vitro fertilization to erectile dysfunction, have become medically treatable there is some sense that truly comprehensive cover-age would include all things that medical interventions can make better.·

• Some of the economic burden of illness has shifted from hos-pitals and the public system to individual citizens. The cost of drugs and home care paid for by individual citizens or their insurers has risen considerably. The greatest out of pocket costs fall on those workers who do not have non-government in-surance coverage. Because concern about one's ability to pay is a major barrier to contact with the health care system, those who are most worried about cost to them, experience exclu-sion from a system which has become less than universal, or find the system less accessible because of these indirect economic barriers. A pediatric oncologist described the impossibility of a middle class family to afford the extra costs associated with a second incidence of cancer in their child. The first brush with cancer had caused them to mortgage their house.

• Each province has dealt with the pressures on the boundaries of coverage in its own fashion. As Health Minister Alan Rock commented at a National Conference on Home Care (1998),

> ... as we look across the country, we see a mixture of long-term, acute and preventive care services. We see some not-for-profit providers, some public-sector involvement and also some commercial and private interests at work. We see that some places administer province-wide projects while others turn authority over to regions to make decisions about delivering home care services. Those regions also sometimes offer a choice of services to be provided. ... We sometimes see different criteria being applied to decide what services a client needs, different health providers for different services and various approaches in determining how much the client should pay. We also see significant private delivery of services.[1]

• The increasing divergence of provincial systems means that someone who is treated for a particular condition under medicare in one province might not be covered in another. This reduces the portability of medicare.

• Private-sector involvement in health care has been increasing in all areas from laboratory services to insurance cover. Perhaps because of pressure on the public purse the shift from public to private funding has already begun. Private payment for health care has gone from about 25% to 35% in the last decade. As private insurers and furnishers of health services, from physiotherapy to PET scans begin to administer a greater proportion of health, :public administration comes under pressure.

Public policy in the area of health care has been remarkably impoverished over the last number of years. The great successes of the past like the introduction of medicare, the publication of the Lalonde Report and the passage of the Canada Health Act have not been achieved in recent years. In fact, if health policy were to be measured by levels of public confidence there has been a steady failure for more than a decade.

The outcomes of health policy interventions are not the only reason to think that health policy has been based on a weak understanding of the nature of health systems and organizations. A much better indication of this failure is the glaring fact that policy makers in different countries have taken diametrically opposite approaches to solve similar problems. While most Canadian provinces were regionalizing their health care systems to eliminate independent institutions with the hope of making the system more efficient, the UK was busy creating independent institutions to foster competition with the expectation that this too would result in increased efficiency. Similarly changes to funding streams indicated the same lack of understanding of the role of finance in health care systems. While the UK was separating the provider function from purchasing of health care, the US was creating vertically integrated health systems where the insurance funders also began to own and control provider organizations. Many of these responses came from ideological commitments either to market forces or to strong regulatory mechanisms. Often the perceived scale of the problems determined the level of response. Hence, there was widespread and massive restructuring of health care systems in the English speaking world. A conference devoted to the consequences of restructuring concluded that that the major result was a widespread destabilization of health care systems. Some argued that the desire for increased efficiency of the system resulted only in economies that were passed from one sector to another - savings in hospitals shifted the burden of cost or care to other providers and consumers of health care.

It is evident that if a sustainable health care system is to emerge it will require a fundamental shift in how we understand and intervene in health care systems. The good news is that innovative ideas about the nature of organizations and systems, planning and policy development have been emerging, but are only now beginning to be understood. Mintzberg and others have suggested that rational strategic planning models need to be rethought in the light of our better understanding of rapidly changing and significantly less-predictable environments.

At Health and Everything, we have spent the last three years immersed in this somewhat conceptual area. Our support from Federal and Provincial Ministries of health, government agencies and private foundations provided a chance to develop some of these ways of thinking and apply them to health. Our results have been published in several places and we have begun to apply this thinking to particular problems. In this paper we suggest some approaches that social democrats might use to resolve the current impasse in health care policy.

A simple distinction between the complicated and the complex can help us understand some of these ideas. Merely complicated problems can be broken down into simpler solvable parts. And once all parts of the problem are solved, the large problem is resolved. Such large difficult problems require careful coordination and resource allocation. Building a bridge and getting a man on the moon are good examples of such problems. The solution can be very complicated, require large amounts of resource and take a very long time. We might say that these problems occur in the context of mechanistic systems. Once they are solved, the solutions become replicable in those systems.

Complex problems are sometimes called "wicked" problems because they have emergent characteristics that cannot be reduced to their constitutive parts. When solved, the solutions do not function as recipes, which can be applied to other, like problems. There a re many good examples of such problems. Often they are problems of prediction. We have learned that there are definite limits to our capacity to predict the weather, the stock market, or indeed, the next drip of the faucet. But they also include problems of how to intervene in complex situations. We know with some precision how to bake a cake, but not how to raise a child. In fact, raising any child may be full of uncertainty, may result in unexpected instability, failure of standardized approaches or surprising successes. The context of these problems has been called complex adaptive systems.

We have argued that that problems relating to health organizations and systems, health policy and health itself are complex rather than complicated problems that occur in the context of complex adaptive systems. The table below lists some of the characteristics of the two kinds of systems.

Interventions in complex adaptive systems require careful consideration and planning but of a different kind than in mechanistic systems. It is more important to understand local conditions and to be aware of the uncertainty that accompanies any intervention. Some

TABLE 1. Complicated Mechanistic and Complex Adaptive Systems

Complicated Systems	Complex Adaptive Systems
Linearity	Non-linearity
Simple causality	Mutual causality
Equilibrium	Non-equilibrium
Reversibility in time	Irreversibility (time's arrow)
Determinism	Probabilistic
Optimization	Satisfaction
Certainty	Uncertainty
Closed systems	Interactive systems
Noise and fluctuations suppressed	Opportunity seen in noise and fluctuations
Averages always dominate	Exceptions dominate near critical thresholds
Asymptotic stability	Structural stability at the edge of chaos
Structural constancy	Evolution/structural change
Analysis/reductionism	Holism/synthesis
Reductive characteristics	Emergent characteristics
Convergent thinking	Divergent thinking
Assumed predictability	Predictability severely limited by instability, structural change, and chaos

preliminary frameworks have organized the thinking about policy interventions in these complex adaptive systems.

Five key elements of such frameworks include

- The need for stability as a counterpart and foundation for change
- The need for a variety of efforts and incremental changes
- The recognition of potential interactions between the constituents of system
- The need to support self-organization as a response to instability
- The need to developing procedures for monitoring and selecting intervention.

These frameworks can be applied to the questions of medicare and healthcare systems, and can act as recommendations for social democrats.

DEVELOP A STABLE CENTRAL STATEMENT OF OBJECTIVES

Stability creates the freedom to change. A critical feature is the need for government to subscribe to and maintain the core values of medicare while at the same time containing costs and achieving a high quality of service. Social democrats are seen to support and understand the basic values and principles associated with medicare because they were instrumental in developing the initial ideas and the first implementation of publicly funded universal health care coverage. In the UK the Labour Party remains the widely accepted protector of the NHS for this reason. In fact, Labour was elected in 1997 without a detailed health policy, but with a strong objective of preserving and improving the NHS. In Canada, medicare is part of the social democratic heritage. Canadians trust social democratic motivations with regard to preserving medicare more than that of more conservative parties.

Social democrats must embrace new ways of thinking about health care systems which recognize that the greatest economies in the system will come from creating and maintaining relatively stable structures and a stable funding flow. Any great change in either of these, we have learned from bitter experience, increases pressure on the system and may, indeed, increase costs and the number of contacts. Creating greater confidence in the system and a belief that it will not be dismantled is a major objective of this stable background.

RECOGNIZE THAT HEALTH AND HEALTH CARE INTERACT WITH OTHER SOCIAL DEMOCRATIC OBJECTIVES

One of the major flaws in health policy is to see health as an end in itself. It interacts with the larger objectives of social justice and well-being. Medicare contributes to these larger objectives not simply by delivering health care to all. It also is an instrument of fair redistribution of resources which is widely approved of by Canadians. (This generosity depends to some extent on the success of the system. It begins to be eroded as the system decays and people fear for their own access.)

Recognizing the interaction between medicare and these other objectives can provide a richer picture of the role of universal coverage. The portability of medicare stands in stark contrast to the American system where workers are tied to their jobs or their location by their current insurance coverage. This lack of portability of health care coverage constrains the independence of individuals and families. There is little doubt that portable health care coverage allows for increased worker mobility and a higher percentage of independent workers in Canada than in the USA.

Because health and health care are so often and carefully measured, the health of the population is not only a good indication of the health care they receive, it is more than likely an excellent indication of the well-being of the population. A social democratic health policy must recognize that health is only one contributor to well-being while measures of health are relatively good indicators of well-being.

RECOGNIZE THE GOOD INTENTIONS OF PROFESSIONALS

Most health professionals enter their fields with altruistic motives. The best and the brightest become doctors not because of the millions they might make but because they hope to do some good. It is also an expectation that they will earn enough money to live as their colleagues do in other countries. In fact there are excellent OECD studies which show that doctors in most developed countries work to targets rather than to achieve extreme wealth. They tend to earn between three and five times the national average wage regardless of the structure of the system and payment mechanisms. The differences between different national groups appear to be narrowing over time despite the growing divergence of health care systems. Assuring doctors of their expected income level can attract them to a shared agenda, which must include increasing public confidence and reducing unnecessary expenditure in the system.

Social democrats are in an excellent position to provide assurance of job security for nurses. There is good evidence that the sought for savings that led to reducing nursing job security were never achieved. Higher costs for agency nursing and the defection of nurses to other kinds of work, or to nursing work in other countries are some of the consequences. A recent effort to bring Canadian nurses back to Ontario was gaining ground, until the government claimed that it would again drastically reduce hospital expenditure. Cost savings in health care occur when a stable, loyal workforce can share a stable social democratic agenda. This was a standard part of the health care system until the 1990s when there was a failure to recognize that nurses loyalty to their employers was also a combination of altruism and the expectation of relative job security. Jittery nurses have a hard time providing good care.

SUPPORT A WIDE VARIETY OF HEALTH-RELATED PROGRAMS

Small incremental changes work best in complex systems. A wide variety of small programs within the objective of a shared agenda of strengthening confidence in medicare while containing its costs have a greater chance of success than massive interventions, as we have learned to our regret in the last number of years. Interventions in complex systems are best introduced incrementally so as not to destabilize excessively a system that works. Allowing for differences in local implementation can increase variation. The creation of CLSCs in Quebec has evolved in this way. It is a centrally proposed program with local variations that respond to the particular communities being served. In health and social policy, an appropriate policy mix of many initiatives is an important way of pursuing large objectives. A good example are the multiple perinatal policies in France or the proposed best policy mix for Children which is the legacy of Suzanne Peters to Canada.

ENCOURAGE AND MAINTAIN MULTIPLE POINTS OF ACCESS FOR HEALTH AND SOCIAL SUPPORT

Part of the problem of emergency rooms in Canada comes from the reduction in the points of access to health and social support. As funding cuts reduced the number and scale of agencies and voluntary organizations that provided such support, people in trouble often had to wait until their condition grew more critical and they could come to the significantly more expensive emergency room (or the police station.) When there is no more money for the organization which provides friendly visits to the elderly, the elderly arrive more frequently to the emergency room. Similarly, stopping the suicide help line increases even more urgent calls for help to police or ambulance services.

The creation of this vicious cycle begins with the erosion of alternative points of access to health support which creates more pressure on emergency rooms. Solving the emergency room crisis involves putting more resources into them and those organizations to which they send patients.

A broad social democratic agenda would reverse this vicious cycle by rebuilding the social infrastructure and thereby reducing the pressure on the fewer and more expensive points of access.

RECOGNIZE POTENTIAL INTERACTIONS

In health care the division of labour in the acquisition of knowledge has been enormously successful. In every area of health research, the creation of more than 100 specialties and subspecialties in Medicine and Nursing has led to breakthroughs. A teaching hospital can have more than 400 different job titles. This differentiation of knowledge and task is a major source of the complexity of a health care organization, because it colours the interactions between providers. Policy initiatives often produce unexpected changes in these interactions. An excellent example of this was the introduction of fund-holding to general practitioners in the UK, which dramatically changed the relationships between GPs and hospital doctors. The joke goes that before fund-holding, GPs would send Christmas cards to hospital doctors to gain their help. After fund-holding, cards began to be sent in the other direction.

A major issue in health care systems is the coordination of patient flow across the many boundaries of disciplinary, departmental and institutional boundaries. This has always occurred across institutional boundaries and is most often based on entrenched practice and informal relationships among practitioners. Good policies build on existing relationships across those boundaries and foster new ones. Changing formal boundaries of organizations, even by eliminating them often disrupts existing interactions and can have the perverse consequence of disrupting the smooth passage of patients though the system.

ENCOURAGE SELF-ORGANIZATION – AN ESSENTIAL CHARACTERISTIC OF COMPLEX SYSTEMS

Elements of complex systems adapt to environmental change, often in unexpected ways. Small local organizations often emerge to support individuals and groups at risk. Self -organization is a common response to conflict, risk and crisis. Policy initiatives must be able to welcome self-organization, by simply not withholding resources. The self- organization of the gay community as a response to the HIV AIDs epidemic is an excellent example of this. The changes in the community itself and the changing attitudes of the public to the gay community are unexpected consequences of these self-organized efforts.

SELECTION IS A NECESSARY FEATURE OF POLICYMAKING IN COMPLEX SYSTEMS

Because many smaller initiatives will fail as well as succeed, a critical role is that of selecting those initiatives that work for reward and expansion and weeding out clear failures if they result in harm. (Because these initiatives should be relatively inexpensive they should be given quite a lot of time to succeed as long as they do no harm.) Strengthening the reward and complaints system has already begun in health care. Greater transparency of services can help strengthen the system. A lesson from litigation lawyers is that good relations between providers and patients reduces stress on the system. A study in the UK about patient waiting lists showed that simply explaining and clarifying delays to patients is a powerful way of reducing anxiety. These kinds of strategies which make more transparent the resources and services of the system to potential users can serve to help regain public confidence in medicare.

A SHORT LAST WORD

This brief attempt to suggest new ways of thinking about health and health care is based on fresh understanding of health and health care as parts of complex adaptive systems. More complete analyses of this kind are described on the web site of Health and Everything which is located at http://www.healthandeverything.org.

---

[1]Health Canada. "National Conference on Home Care, Proceedings." Halifax: Health Canada, 1998.

Rethinking Principles and Reality in Health Care Reform

EARL BERGER

"One does not discover new lands without consenting to be out of sight of the shore for a very long time."
             — André Gide

Every system is perfectly designed to achieve exactly the results it gets.
   — Dr. Donald Berwick, Institute for Health Improvement

ONE THING IS CLEAR. THE GREAT SUCCESS OF SOCIAL democracy in Canada is the embodiment in federal and provincial legislation of the principles of The *Canada Health Act*: universality, accessibility, comprehensiveness, portability and public administration. With two major exceptions - medication and dental care, social democratic principles are the foundation of health care in Canada.

  And yet it is not enough for social democrats to merely maintain and uphold the *Act.* Rather, we must better grasp it's underlying principles and imagine ways to keep these in force. In fact, the *Canada Health Act* gives us much more room to manouevre and extends many more opportunities for creativity than some social democrats have realized. We need to avoid reflex and routine proposals and we need to think more deeply and critically about how best to maintain our health care principles into the 21st century.

The argument in this paper is uncomfortable. There is no defined end or perfect system of health care; there is only an on-going debate and a process of reform. For its part the process must constantly provide new incentives for health care professionals and it must discover ways to encourage providers to reach for higher levels of community health and well being - that as well as vigilantly treating illness. As it stands today, the health care community is reimbursed primarily for treating illness and is hard pressed to attend to the general health of our population. Reform must take us in the latter direction and it is in the details of the existing processes that we can find opportunities to do so.

CANADIANS WANT REFORM

The Health Care System is the first priority of Canadians. Not only do Canadians want the principles of the *Act* to remain in full force[1], but they are worried about the quality of health care and they are worried that access to care is becoming more difficult. Canadians are prepared for health care reform: 80% or more consistently support patient rostering and[2] similar percentages support multidisciplinary health practices.

Reform does not mean adopting a more American like health care system. Studies in the United States and elsewhere have demonstrated that users fees and two-tier payment programs, discourage the use of necessary health services among the poor, do nothing to discourage inappropriate use of services, do not generate significant savings to health care, and often end up costing much more[3]. Moreover, the argument that a two-tier service relieves demand on the public sector health system makes no sense where physicians, nurses, imaging technicians and other service providers are in short supply. Removing some of them from the public sector to fee-for-service does nothing to alleviate overall supply shortages, and it diminishes the resources available to the public sector.

SHORTAGES

First, we must recognize that, because of demographics, we are in a life-long competition for physicians, nurses and other health care resources. Some shortages of health personnel would be alleviated if those who were foreign-trained were able to obtain their licenses to practice more speedily, and if programs were put in place to assist them with their English or French language capabilities. These responsibilities lie with the provincial regulatory Colleges. The federal and provincial governments could do more to facilitate the processes of integration by assistance to the immigrant health professionals and to the Colleges in assessing credentials. This is a natural task for social democrats.

But, the issues are not simply American and now British agencies offering our health care providers more money. Money alone is not normally enough to tempt providers and their families away from Canada. We lose health care providers more because of the obstacles to improving the working environment than because of money. Providers are committed to their vocation and want reform. But when doctors and nurses find themselves enmeshed in a tangle of customs, prejudices, rules, regulations, animosities and budgetary issues they become frustrated and sometimes see no way to stay put.

To open up discussions about health care reform, we begin with the four informal laws to which any health care reform in Canada must adhere.

a. We need to create health care systems. People talk about the health care system as if there was one, but one cannot call something a system when whoever has a truck, can make up their own routes, and deliver services wherever and whenever they wish for as long or short a period as they want[4].

Over the past two decades every provincial government has devoted great energy to attempting to shape the variety of informal and semi-formal arrangements among its various health providers and institutions into some kind of system with some capacity for governance, management, fiscal responsibility and accountability.

b. Health care needs to be about health as well as illness: There is no body, agency or group with the responsibility for both illness and health. No one has a financial incentive to create a healthy society, except the taxpayer, who is also the spender. There have been noble efforts - e.g. public health authorities, smoking cessation and nutrition programs - in the direction of healthy communities. But, no one has succeeded in tying these efforts to illness-treatment services. The latter have absorbed most of our energies and thinking.

c. *Health care does not mean buildings.* We need to say this every night before we go to bed. Some hospitals provide poor care; some hospital duplicate care available several blocks away. The money spent on unnecessary buildings and their maintenance is huge. For example, one community hospital in Toronto fought for 20 years to remain open even though the services it offered were available just a few blocks away at a teaching hospital. This community hospital received approximately $25 million a year; if we assume $10 million of that was spent on keeping the building open, the cost to the health system was $200 million, a sum with which we could have paid for all the MRIs and digital mammography equipment we need. Closing hospitals can be good for health care[5]. The principles of social democracy should not be confused with sentiment.

d. *The objectives of health care reform cannot be laid out in advance; reform resides in the process itself.* Even to those of us who are "experts" in the field wisdom comes hard and we realize what works only via exploration and then only for the local circumstances. In the current phraseology "visibility is limited". We do not know what the "there" is in health care reform. And with the end undefined the journey "there" becomes de facto health care reform. Rethinking health care thus involves ways of incorporating local change into systems that meet the principles of the *Canada Health Act.*

MONEY

Something else is also clear. The long-term solution to our current difficulties is not putting more money into our current health care arrangements. In 1998, Canadians' total spending on health care was almost $3,000 per capita, fifth among 27 OECD countries[6]. The United States spends the most (close to $4,500) and has the worst public health record - high infant mortality rate, high percentages of uninsured and underinsured. The chart below indicates roughly the relationship between expenditures on health care and quality of care (considered in terms of appropriate care for the specified condition).

As the chart indicates, at some point increased expenditures on health care do not achieve much in the way of overall improvements in the quality of health care. What is surprising is that the figure was about $900 a year (CDN), or about $1,300 per capita today.

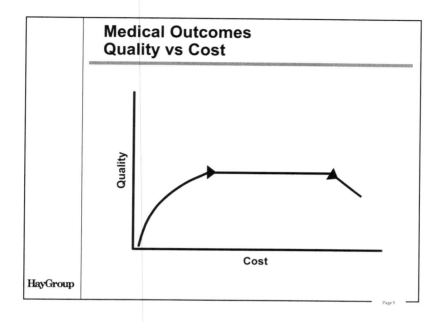

**Medical Outcomes
Quality vs Cost**

HayGroup

Page 5

Unquestionably, Canada suffers from persistent capital under funding over the past two decades. In fact capital needs are so pressing and public pressure so great it is hard for governments to refrain from spending on capital improvements even though they realize that, without long-term system improvements, spending will result in less than optimal results. Obvious difficult choices include government funding for hospitals which should have merged or closed years ago, and for the regular, seasonal "emergency room overcrowding" crises which have little to do with the emergency room itself.

There are two challenges that social democrats must face. One is to create a health system which is, in fact, a system, and which is amenable to effective management, accountability and quality control. The second challenge is to build into this health system the financial incentives to encourage health as well as treat illness. Should a social democratic party take on these challenges successfully the results will translate into increased electoral support.

The remaining portion of this chapter examines one effort to create a new illness treatment-health promotion system in one community. The issues may seem local; the implications, however, are much broader.

171

The Willett, for those readers who do not recall the 1970's headlines, is a small hospital in Paris, Ontario. The Willett's story was similar to that of many small hospitals across the country: It could not match the clinical expertise and experience in the larger hospitals, few people used its acute care services, a dentist used the operating rooms once or twice a week. The late Frank Miller, then Ontario Minister of Health, travelled to Paris to propose closing the hospital. He was pelted and the tires on his aide's car were slashed. Those were deeply radical acts in small town Ontario and talk of closing The Willett was off the agenda. But the problems inherent in running The Willet remained.

In 1996, a far-sighted local group came to us for help. Their idea was to transform The Willett into a community health and well being centre. Physicians, nurses, nutritionists, physiotherapists and other health and wellness services would be provided. As health care consultants we were certain that success depended on the physicians cooperation because they were critical to health care delivery. If the doctors would support the venture it would work, and if not, the venture had little chance of success.

The Willet group retained us to take what was then a radical project forward, and from this unlikely beginning one of the more successful attempts at primary care reform in Ontario was on its way.

The following provides a general description of some of the many issues that arose in the process of reforming and transforming The Willet. I present these issues not in any order of priority.

INTEGRATION

The Willett group were looking for an "integrated health system" at the community level. One of the first questions was: what and who gets "integrated". Would it be:

- Services and programs, eg community care, long-term care services, home care services, hospital services;

OR

- The providers, physicians, nurses, physiotherapists;

OR

- The larger institutions eg, the hospital, the nursing homes, the rehabilitation centres.

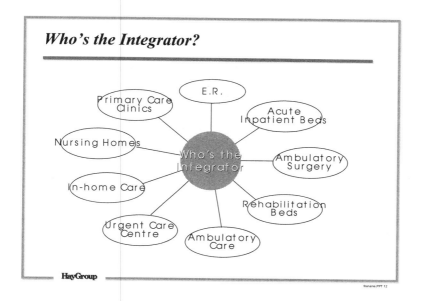

And what did "integration" mean?

> • Cooperation or collaboration — formal agreements among the various parties to cooperate or collaborate with each other;
> • Coordination — agreement to set up a coordinating function among all the health providers, which means, in practical terms, some loss of autonomy for each of the participants;
> • Delegation or transfer of responsibilities — agreement that the responsibilities of some entities would be delegated or transferred to other entities;
> • System Governance Models — agreement to set up a governing body for all the entities to direct their activities;
> Mergers or new types of organizations to include the hospitals, nursing homes, physicians and other providers.

These questions raised profound issues of professional scope of practice and autonomy, governance, fiscal accountability, legal responsibilities, contract law as well as the provision of health services. Because the process took place within a community these issues became personal and immediate rather than abstract. The only way to deal with the issues was face to face with the community, taking each complexity and working through the details. If we and the community were to be successful, we had no other choice.

THE WILLETT AS INTEGRATOR

Every health care system needs an integrator, an agency or group which holds it all together, handles the coordination of resources and funding, handles core administrative activities etc. One proposal was that the integrator of choice should be someone at the centre of community health. The hospital for its part should remain in the second or third circle, merely a resource for acute health situations[7]. But The Willett, though it was technically a hospital, was for all practical purposes already a community health centre. The community's "hospital" was not The Willett but the hospital in Brantford.

COMPENSATION - THE HEART OF THE MATTER

One of the hardest things for social democrats to deal with in health care reform is the role of financial incentives in shaping the effective delivery of services. To be fair, not even the corporations always get it.

This chart may seem obvious, but in reality compensation in health care usually runs in the opposite direction to health care reform.

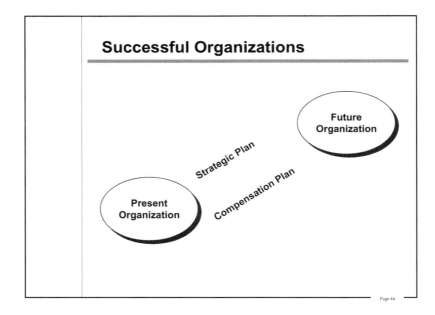

Canada has two basic compensation arrangements for physicians. Some physicians are on straight salary. Most physicians prefer to work on a fee-for-service basis. The more patients a physician sees the greater the physician's income and the greater the burden on the public purse. The physician is paid when she treats illness, not when she helps patients and the community to stay healthy (there are exceptions but they only emphasize the pervasiveness of the fee-for-illness treatment model).

Hospitals have a different model. They receive global funding to support their operating plan[8]. Those hospitals rewarded with additional funding are those that run over budget. Corporations can close a badly-run factory. Governments find it difficult to close a hospital without potentially harming the community if the hospital is the only one in town. Hospitals that stay within their budgets get the usual annual funding increase. The hospital's incentive, therefore, is to run over budget, go into deficit and beg for lots more funding[9].

One effort to put compensation and health reform under one roof has been to establish regional health authorities with regional budgets for the various providers. This approach, so far, has had two shortcomings. On the one hand , physicians object to being controlled in this way. They often fight to remain outside the regional authority, on a fee-for-service basis; they have no financial stake in establishing a healthy community or in helping the other providers under the regional authority do so. Again, if government pays a provider only to treat illness then it cannot nor should not expect them to spend time putting themselves out of business. What financial incentives to create a healthy community do physicians who are paid to treat sick people have? Their professional ethics move them to promote health, but their compensation plan moves them in the opposite direction.

The second drawback, to the regional health authority approach, is that the providers within the regional authority - the hospitals, long-term care facilities, rehabilitation clinics, and so on - are not rewarded if, in fact, they do improve community health. Most often the money saved is diverted to the less efficient, the poorly managed and the fiscally irresponsible. We need to find ways in which health care providers have at least some financial incentives to keep communities healthy.

At the The Willett, there were 8 physicians in the hospital's catchment area of about 19,000 people. Approximately half of the physicians worked in Paris. The others worked in small communities nearby.

Most of the physicians had small practices which produced reasonable incomes and that suited them. As one doctor said " it leaves me time to fly my plane". Meetings with the physicians made it plain that they would participate in primary care reform if three conditions were met: 1. if they could improve the professional quality of their services; 2. if they could improve their own quality of life (working hours, time with families); and 3. if they would neither be degraded or lose income.

Negotiations began on setting up a group practice with a "roster" of patients. The group practice would include all the physicians, and the roster would include everyone in the community. The physicians would receive a lump sum, or capitation fee, for the roster. The capitation fee would be adjusted to account for the age and condition of the patients - for example, a higher capitation rate for seniors. The capitation fee would be used to pay for all the health and related services, including hospital services, that the community would need.

With the capitation fee, the physician could decide upon the most cost-effective ways to treat patients and to keep them healthy. The physician might, for example, use dietitians and trainers to work with obese and diabetic community members. Because a physician was responsible for overall patient management she could spend her time addressing the broader issues of community health. The hypothesis we used was this: A healthier community uses less health care services. It thereby uses less of the capitation fee which is not returned to the government but left as incentive to physicians and to other health care providers. This model is referred to as "aligning the compensation plan with the overall strategy".

The U.S. experience has revealed drawbacks to the capitation fee. If fee-for-service tends to increase health service use, capitation tempts the physician to increase their net revenues by reducing their services to patients, or by declining to take on patients with complex and expensive chronic conditions such as HIV/AIDs or dementia. In the United States, patients are limited to their health plans which means they cannot switch physicians at will; they can use only the physicians in their plan.

Our thinking was that in Canada, where patients could if they were getting less than adequate care the fear of losing patients, and thus capitation fees, would keep physicians and other health care providers eager to provide good quality care[10].

Health Care Expenses. One task was to address the physicians' expenses. An analysis of provincial data indicated that for Brant County, where The Willet was located, annual per capita health care expenditures were[11]:

Line Item	Average Annual Per Capita Expenditure
Acute Inpatient & Day Surgery (secondary)	$386
Acute Inpatient & Day Surgery (tertiary)	$79
Acute Outpatient	$126
Sub-Total: Acute Care Services	$591
Chronic Care Services	$145
Rehab Inpatient	$18
Rehab Outpatient	$6
Physician Services	$325
Drug Costs	$82
Home Care	$92
Missing pieces:	
Community programs (OHIP funded)	$21 est
Lab Services (OHIP funded)	$59 est
Total	$1,339

One of the objectives of primary care reform was to shift more of the burden to the family physician or general practitioner and away from the more expensive medical specialist. The typical split in provincial expenditures for physicians at that time was 40% for GPs and 60% for the specialists. We estimated that the GPs could do more of the work and that the $325 split fee would be 50%/50% or, after adjustments, approximately $146 per patient for GP services.

Given the caseloads the cardiologists in the area already had, this income shifting was not a major issue. But, it could be with other specialists and in other contexts. Decisions regarding who provides what service, quite rightly raise the concerns of the medical specialists about both reduced incomes and about the capabilities of GPs to provide services for which they may not be properly trained.

NET INCOME

The Paris GPs billed OHIP an average of $180,000 a year. Given that their per capita funding was $146 per patient this meant that they would need approximately 1,230 patients on their roster to maintain their incomes, which is about what most of them had.

But, if the physicians were organized into a group practice, and some of them moved into The Willett, which would handle their office and administrative responsibilities on a shared cost basis, they could reduce their expenses and thus increase their take-home revenue. A New Brunswick study found that GPs earned on average about $180,000 a year, but spent more than 40% of that on rent, staff and other overhead. This pattern is similar for most physicians in solo practice.

But, with a "group" practice centred on The Willet, each physician saved about $13,000 a year in expenses. In other words they could increase their net revenues without increasing their fees, and they would have more money to spend on "healthy community" activities. They would also provide savings in the form of reduced fees to medical specialists, and fewer hospital stays due to improved preventive care.

This approach seemed tidy, but difficulties soon arose. Some physicians had office leases or offices in their home; some paid their spouses to handle the office administration. It took many meetings for these issues to be resolved. But in the final analysis they were resolved.

RISK

The physicians were concerned that the capitation fee of $146 per rostered patient would not cover the expenses of providing both illness treatment and "healthy community" services. They were willing to accept some risk, but wanted assurances from the Ministry that they would be protected against unlimited risk. By now, we were into our second year of discussions.

The Ministry of Health, also new to rostering[12], was reluctant to guarantee physician losses. The physicians agreed to set aside their financial concerns if the Ministry would send them a "comfort letter" in which it promised to make best efforts to ensure that the physicians did not suffer financially. A letter from the Ministry did eventually arrive but offered nothing but, 'Thanks for your cooperation and have a good trip'. This was enough for the physician and primary care reform in Paris was on its way.

It is too early to say how things will work out in Paris. Many of those who created the reform process have moved on and those that remained may now have different concepts about The Willett as an integrator and as a community wellness centre.

Though The Willett process took place under a Conservative government with a reputation for cutting tax and services it represents a process that social democrats ought to embrace. The model - based on local process tied to the principles of the *Canada Health Act* - emphasized the interests and values of the community and its stakeholders and the long-term objectives of ensuring health services and supporting a healthy community.

THE UNION

If one wants the hospital included as part of a model in which the health providers are responsive to community needs, then among all the other issues to be addressed is the one that strikes at the soul of social democracy - the union.

In Canada, hospital workers are heavily unionized and for good reason. Many hospitals over the past decades have treated professional and support staff badly. One result has been a work environment bound by rules, procedures and legislated processes. Collective bargaining was intended to provide protection to hospital staff but sometimes the results obstruct other more flexible alternatives better suited to local conditions.

It is not, of course, that hospital staff does not need or deserve protection. It is that both the hospital and the union would have to redefine what the purpose of that protection is and how it would be expressed in a community setting where responsiveness and flexibility to local needs are the primary prerequisites.

To raise the union question is to open the discussion to a slew of highly contentious issues:

- Should a union be entitled to restrict the ways health services are organized and delivered in a community (assuming decent working conditions)?
- Is it reasonable to expect that a union, or any organization, would voluntarily give up its place in a hospital?
- Who will fight for flexible responses to community needs, preferences and values?
- If the union and community health providers come to an agreement in one setting, would the union agree that another agreement would be suitable in another setting?
- Will a social democratic party stand up for community needs or for the demands of the union?
- Is there enough trust among the parties that this kind of discussion is even possible?

CENTRAL ISSUES OF HEALTH CARE REFORM

Efforts to reform health care in the provinces must deal with similar questions to those we faced in dealing with The Willett.

Social democrats must accept that a health system will work best when all the stakeholders have financial, professional, personal and community incentives moving them in the same direction. One of the most difficult matters we need to explore is just how to balance compensation, risk and (appropriate) incentives for the health providers with the service needs of the population, and the limited resources available to the government.

We must also take notice of the smelly elephant that just dumped in our living room. The events of September 2001 remind us that health care is not simply about being healthy and caring for the ill. Health care is also part of the front line against bio-terrorism and warfare. Health care is part of national defense, indeed of global defense. A colleague remarked recently of a conference of 1,800 infectious disease specialists from around the world - if the terrorists had crashed into that conference the world would have been helpless to identify or protect itself from bio-warfare. Infectious disease specialists are far harder to find than are investment counsellors, money managers and Pentagon workers.

The dangers of bio-terrorism create a different context for health care: physicians and nurses as unarmed front line soldiers where the front line is home. These dangers change the health care reform dynamic greatly. They place profound importance upon public health, protection and early warning - again with appropriate incentives to make health care congruent with defense.

---

[1]For example, between 80% to almost 100% of Canadians think each of the principles of the Canada Health Act is important. *The Berger Population Health Monitor*, Survey #21, May 2000.

[2]*Ibid.*

[3]Some U.S. states tried to reduce Medicaid costs by limiting the number of prescriptions per senior per month. In response, physicians admitted poor seniors to nursing homes and hospitals where the medications were provided and from which, because of the "institutional effect" many patients did not leave. The overall result was higher costs to the state. Some states stopped paying for benzodiazepines because of concerns over overuse. This led to increased use of sedatives which were potentially more toxic and more costly I am indebted to Stephen Soumerai, Harvard University, for these and other examples of unintended effects.

[4]The analogy was made by Dr. Martin Barkin, former Ontario Deputy Minister of Health. The defining moment for system building in Ontario came when Dr. Barkin's Minister, Elinor Caplan, was criticized because a man had died after spending 18 months on the waiting list for a heart valve operation. In fact, neither Ms. Caplan *nor the hospital* had any say in the waiting list. The deceased's place on the waiting list, as was customary at the time, was the decision of his physician who put the patient on the waiting list to give him hope even though he was not an appropriate candidate for heart valve surgery - which is why he never moved up the list. The furor, although it was widely misunderstood at the time, galvanized the Minister into creating the beginnings of what became Ontario's cardiac care network, which in turn was a model for the province's cancer care network and for other provincial care coordinating agencies. Out of such misunderstandings health system improvements can occur.

[5]When the NDP government in Saskatchewan closed rural hospitals across the province, there was an outcry about the economic and health care implications. Whatever the economic implications of the closures, the indications are that health outcomes improved following the closures. It may have been more inconvenient for people to travel from their community to a larger city hospital, but the clinical staff and equipment were better and so were patient outcomes.

[6]"Health Care in Canada: 2001", Canadian Institute for Health Information, Statistics Canada, Ottawa, 2001p. 71 et seq. Many of the four spend more public dollars than Canada.

[7]"If you look at what is happening in California, it is clear that the hospital is not the center of the emerging healthcare delivery system. Where the center is exactly, may vary from place to place within the state, but it is clearly somewhere inside the physician community." Goldsmith, Jeff, "The Illusive Logic of Integration", *Healthcare Forum Journal*, September/October 1994.

[8]Plus special, one-time and fee-for-service funding. The complexities of hospital funding strain explanation.

[9]This routine may be losing its effectiveness. Ontario replaced The Ottawa Hospital's board because of its annual budget overruns. Since board members are volunteers, their punishment is embarrassment.

[10]More practically, many in rural and small town Canada are already effectively rostered because there are few physicians to choose from.

[11]1966 data, amounts are approximate.

[12]The Ministry, again under a Conservative government, had tried something like this years before, but it had been labelled as "communist" or "socialist" by many of the local doctors who refused to participate.

An Urban Vision for an Urban Party

JORDAN BERGER

Urban life muddles through the pace of history. When this pace accelerates, cities - and their people - become confused, spaces turn threatening, and meaning escapes from experience. In such disconcerting yet magnificent times, knowledge becomes the only source to restore meaning, and thus meaningful action.[1]

Innovation, or the flow of new knowledge, thrives in an environment of collaboration, but dies in an environment based solely on competition.[2]

As a displaced Newfoundlander, I begin with an apology to my fellow Canadians. I live in Toronto.

Like most people who hail from what Central Canadians' cheerfully term "the regions," I arrived in Toronto with a healthy dose of resentment towards the city. Expecting to see herds of white, Anglo-Saxon, self-important, obscenely wealthy, cold colonialists I stepped on to a subway car packed with every race, religion, and creed known to humankind.

This was the beginning of my education in the diversity that marks our largest cities. With time, I have come to love Toronto - its energy, distinct neighborhoods, global influences, eclectic architecture, and talented, creative people. As well, I share the concerns of many of my neighbours and friends regarding the growing poverty and homelessness that is concentrated in the city, developments that are encouraged by a provincial government that favours the suburbs over the inner core. Over the years, my early assumptions about the city have faded and I have grown to appreciate its complexities, internal disparities, diversity, and constantly changing population.

The gap between one's conception of the city and its reality is surely found in all Canadian provinces. Growing up as a child in St. John's - the metropolis of Newfoundland - the same divisions existed between misunderstood urbanite and the rest of the province. It is the curse of cities to be envied and despised. Few politicians who represent non-urban ridings, and fewer still who operate at the level of provincial or national politics recognize and support publicly the contribution cities make to our society and economy.

In this chapter, I argue that the NDP can and should be the champion of urban issues. The NDP needs an *urban vision* that is both grand - to excite the emotions - and specific - providing solid solutions to real urban problems. Most Canadians live in cities and increasingly recognize their local neighborhoods, communities, and networks as the key areas for engagement and activism. The NDP must recognize the growing importance of urban areas - where its electoral base and future lie - and reach urban voters where they live. While most of the examples below are based on Toronto, the arguments can be applied by others to urban centres from coast to coast.

REDEFINING SOCIAL DEMOCRACY

The New Democratic Party faces a huge challenge - to become relevant once again by articulating our long-held principles and policies in a manner that makes sense and matters to most Canadians. Given our increasing electoral marginality, it is clear that we have so far failed this test.

Like most losing political activists, New Democrats take solace from the conviction that most Canadians support our beliefs. And, polling data indicates that a great deal more voters support basic social democratic principles than are willing to vote for us.

What is our social democratic agenda? Although Party members are currently engaged in a wide-ranging debate about our policies, internal structure, and basic identity, there are certain enduring principles that will remain the heart of everything we do. These include: valuing people over profits, citizenship before consumerism, communities over unregulated markets, diversity over conformity, and solidarity over self-centred individualism.

While we may take some comfort from the recitation of such common-sense principles, it is also evident that our articulation of these general goals is not influencing the voting patterns of our fellow citizens. Our rhetoric is dated and stale, our internal debates too picayune and obscure, and our vision of a better Canada too disconnected from the reality of life in a changing country and world.

Fortunately, voters no longer expect their political parties to inspire. In the absence of a stirring vision, voters demand only that politicians explain what they want to do, how they will pay for it, and how they will ensure that Canadians benefit from change, rather than become the victims of change. This raises another daunting obstacle for the NDP, our lack of an economic analysis that recognizes how wealth is created and that assures average citizens the resources will be there to accomplish all of the good things we collectively support.

In his autobiography, *The Good Fight*, David Lewis uses the words of a British academic, John Wilson, to sum up the challenge faced by the left in a prosperous country like Canada, "The demand for permanent social reform... seems precisely to be born of the natural human inclination to consider the quality of one's life only after one's basic material needs are being met. But simply because of the prosperity which that condition represents, the demand for change is always made in a conservative way."[3] For too long, the NDP has been content to ignore economic issues and has failed to see the intimate connection between popular support for state policies of redistribution and their concern about the economic well-being of themselves, their families, and their communities.

The answer to the challenges outlined above is for the Party to engage in a real way with the emerging reality of city life and to draw the links - increasingly apparent at the urban level - between economic growth, environmental sustainability, and social solidarity.

But first, I want to touch on the role urban issues did *not* play in our recent federal campaign.

CAMPAIGN 2000: A MISSED OPPORTUNITY

Most New Democrats will be surprised by the statement that the last Federal NDP platform offered a new deal for Canada's cities. For example, the Party made major commitments to a national strategy for public housing, generous federal funding of public transit and passenger rail, environmental investment in green industries, environmental retrofitting of municipal and private buildings, rehabilitation of abandoned industrial lands, and tax incentives to support new media. More importantly, however, the Party formally acknowledged the role urban areas should play in national politics by offering a seat for Canada's urban communities in future federal conferences and negotiations.

Sadly, none of the above amounted to anything more than good intentions. Although these were heartfelt commitments, the federal platform did not bring these disparate proposals together into an urban vision. Neither was there any effort to empower urban candidates to do so.

Finally, as some New Democrats have wryly commented, health care was, in 2000, the "monster that swallowed our Party." While it is certainly true that in today's media-driven campaigns, there is little space for complicated messages, voters expect to be taken seriously. Our campaign, however, was limited to a simple mantra of "health care, health care, health care."

An expressly urban platform would have been a unique contribution to the 2000 campaign and one with which the other parties would have a hard time engaging. The Canadian Alliance's rural base and small-minded obsession with market solutions to all social problems are out of step with the reality of urban life. And the governing Liberal Party could have been made a victim of its own success - how would it have countered a NDP strategy targeting downtown ridings with an urban platform without jeopardizing its candidates in the rest of the country?

Ironically, the leader who came closest to tapping the urban sensibility was Joe Clark and his audacious campaign to win Calgary Centre. In this quintessentially urban riding, Clark's team built an unlikely coalition of Liberals, New Democrats, Conservatives, gays, artists, and other city dwellers. His victory preserved a measure of political diversity in national politics and the desire for new voices and expanded political choices corresponds well to the diversity that increasingly characterizes big city life.

In summary, on the cusp of a new millennium in which the importance of cities in the new economy can only increase, the New Democratic Party failed to translate its good intentions on urban issues into a winning formula. The NDP did not speak to the profound challenges facing our cities and missed its opportunity to stand alone, among the major parties, in providing a strong urban vision.

CANADA'S FUTURE IS URBAN

Today, four of every five Canadians lives in urban areas. Almost two out of three live in one of Canada's 25 city-regions with populations in excess of 100,000. One in three live in Toronto, Vancouver, or Montréal. The urbanization of our society continues apace with growing urban sprawl balanced by increasingly dense residential development in city cores. Rural areas are also becoming home to knowledge workers using technology to combine a rural setting with work destined for urban markets.

Why does this shift in settlement patterns matter? Cities are emerging as the key nodes of a global economy - as well as the key sites for those who promote social democratic concerns and international solidarity over the short-term capital flows that drive corporate globalization.

Struggles to humanize trade, to repatriate popular control over trade rules and corporations, and to ensure human diversity in the face of consumer homogenization, will continue and the Party needs to be at the forefront of these battles. However, what is also inescapably true is that Canada has moved beyond the relatively self-centred economic model of the post-war era and our national origins as a trading nation have re-emerged. To take Toronto as one example among many, the city's exports to the rest of Canada in 1981 were roughly equivalent to its exports to the rest of the world. In 1995, exports outside Canada are worth almost three times internal exports.[4]

Canada is a quintessential trading nation - from the fur and fish that drove European expansion in the 17th and 18th centuries to the exploitation of natural resources like nickel, coal, wood, hydroelectric power, potash, and agricultural land that shaped 19th and 20th century industrialization, immigration, and settlement patterns. In this context, the increasing importance of international trade today represents a return to our heritage rather than the final chapter in our national history.

The NDP - like the CCF before it - traditionally focused on trade issues. Our Party has always struggled to assert popular control over economic development, an eminently sensible position in a nation so dominated by external forces, so that all Canadians can share the fruits of our collective labour. The long-term goals that inform our movement have not shifted, but the terrain on which we are active certainly has and our strategic arguments must shift to reflect new realities.

Historically, the Party has been deeply affected by economic change. During the 19th century, many European immigrants either brought a commitment to socialism to their new land or had it drummed into them by oppressive employers, financiers, and trading relationships. Key centres of early CCF activity were the one-industry mining towns of British Columbia, Ontario, and Atlantic Canada. And, of course, our origins and greatest successes were generated by the waves of immigration that established the farming communities of the Prairies.

This was followed, in the post-World War II period, by thousands of immigrants fleeing the poverty of Southern Europe. Many of these new citizens were communists and socialists in their homelands and, to the extent they were actively recruited into the NDP, they injected a new progressive vitality into our Party.

Furthermore, unlike earlier waves of immigration, these newcomers settled primarily in our major cities. They did so because of industrialization, the job opportunities it created, and the many spin-off effects of rapid, urban economic growth. Industrialization brought with it the increasing prominence of cities as sites of power (banks, legislatures, mass advertising and mass media) and of production (the factory). In cities, living standards improved over time as a burgeoning labour movement extracted better wage from employers.

With the deracialization of our immigration policy, our cities are being transformed by huge numbers of immigrants from around the globe, seeking a better world within our borders. Many of these immigrants bring a commitment to progressive politics every bit as rich and historically rooted as our own. The frustrations these immigrants face because of racism, a lack of opportunities, and professional associations that exclude credentials earned overseas, should be a source of new energy for the NDP.

Embracing human diversity has always been a principle, if not always a practice, of the New Democratic Party. In the future, we must broaden our understanding of the concept. Economic diversity, for example, should be encouraged. Too often the NDP has denigrated small business - influenced in large part by private-sector unions - however, small and medium businesses contribute the bulk of employment growth in Canada and provide commercial diversity and local vitality in many urban neighbourhoods. In the same way that the union movement is rethinking its approach to organizing the new workforce, we must rethink our approach to organizing the new electorate. Both are changing in response to the new economy.

While the industrialization that drove urban growth has largely faded, the pressures for geographical convergence are actually growing, not disappearing. New literature on the economic role of location suggests that quality of life issues in urban areas are central to national competitiveness. The promotion of sustainable economic growth and the protection of social solidarity in the face of growing disparities are issues with which the NDP can and should engage. But to do this, we need to recognize some of the drivers of the new economy and some of the pitfalls they present for Canadian society. Again, the arena within which these challenges and counter-challenges will be articulated is an urban one.

CITIES AND THE NEW ECONOMY

Cities provide the bulk of Canada's cultural and artistic output, they provide most of our employment, are the centres for key public services including universities, colleges, and hospitals, and they generate most tax revenues for all levels of government. Our cities face common challenges with large and growing numbers of poor and homeless, new immigrants seeking to contribute and prosper, and the many problems associated with unplanned development. In addition, our cities are being transformed by the requirements and possibilities of the new economy. Recent changes in the global and Canadian economies contain positive and negative implications for our society and, subsequently, our party.

First, the key drivers of the new economy are based less on resource extraction or large-scale manufacturing and more on services, information technology, and other knowledge-intensive industries. Where the old economy used capital investment to deskill workers and drive their wages down, workers in the new economy are increasingly valued for their skills, education, and creativity.

Second, the knowledge economy has a geographic base: today, economic innovation and production increasingly happens in relatively constrained regions and only flourishes through the constant interaction of firms and their employees aided by active state support and strong educational facilities. It is one of the paradoxes of our era that, as one observer puts it, "despite the advent of globally-organized economic activity and the increasingly widespread use of the Internet and other forms of information and communications technology, innovation and knowledge-intensive production have become *more*, not *less*, geographically concentrated, above all in city-regions. In short city-regions have become key nodes in the production and flow of ideas."[5]

As early as 1961, Canadian urbanist Jane Jacobs wrote about the strong relationship between urban creativity and economic growth.[6] An imaginative population often produces the innovations that will later be developed and marketed economically. Jacobs, in her masterpiece, *Cities and the Wealth of Nations*, points out that economic forces rarely drive that innovation. Necessity is not, she argues, always the mother of invention. Many of the inventions that are integral to modern economies - from metallurgy to fabric dying, hydraulics, lathes, cast iron, the chemical industry, the movable type press, plastics, electroplating, and the railroad - were created to satisfy very human qualities like curiosity, esthetics, and the need for entertaining diversions.

To create new innovations, and feed a virtuous cycle of adaptation and economic growth, the proper urban environment must be maintained. As Cyril Stanley Smith comments, "All big things grow from little things, but new little things are destroyed by their environments unless they are cherished for reasons more like esthetic appreciation than practical utility."[7] The urban arena must be shaped so that artistic energies are encouraged and adapted. The link between the arts and economic vitality should be seen as an organic, complex relationship rather than the neoliberal model which values only direct marketability and attacks state supports for creativity.

Finally, the new economy is powered by technology and, in many senses, the technological paradigm now affects all aspects of modern life - from production and consumption, management and work, culture, communication, and education, to genetic engineering, which applies programming techniques to the basic components of human life.[8] The development of weapons of mass destruction, the moral implications of genetic engineering, and the mounting evidence that the planet can not sustain unplanned economic and technological growth are all aspects of an increasingly complex world that requires political engagement rather than trite sloganeering.

THE NEW URBAN ADVANTAGE

But what about the contrast between the inner core of our cities - where urban life is at its most exciting, innovative, and diverse - and the suburbs where so many technology companies are located? Is a technology-savvy vision a suburban one? Is growth limited to, in the words of Kotkin and DeVol, the "suburban nerdistans"?

One need only consider the growth of Silicon Valley to recognize the urban sprawl encouraged by technology-driven growth. However, much of this growth was related to the technical aspects of the technological revolution - the nuts and bolts, software, switches, processors, and scientific and engineering talent that have laid the foundations for the information age. As new technologies are distributed more widely throughout society and people use these technologies to "plug in", the creative aspects of the revolution are becoming more important - and this trend, with its roots in arts and culture, advertising, graphic design and architecture, favours the inner city.

In assessing the information economy, Kotkin and DeVol draw an important distinction between its hard face - the infrastructure of the information age which is highly technical and dominated by the sciences and engineering - and its soft face - the content that travels this infrastructure. This division has, "created a split in the geography of the digital economy. The "hard" side, including activities such as the development [and] production of fiber optics and chips, remains concentrated in the nerdistans of the periphery. The "soft"

191

side, focused primarily on such fundamentally creatively driven fields as media, fashion, advertising and design, has taken on a decidely more urban cast."[9]

The opportunities for cultural expression are concentrated so heavily in urban areas for a variety of reasons. These include expanded educational and training opportunities, a diversity of entertainment and cultural facilities, and, most interestingly, the diversity of human experience, quality of life, and sense of community that attracts talented, creative workers.

Richard Florida of Carnegie Mellon University has sought to quantify the links between the quality of life, diversity, and tolerance found in cities on the one hand and the rise of high-technology industries on the other. In one article, Florida develops what he calls the "bohemian index" - a ranking of American cities by the number of artists, writers, designers, musicians and composers, actors and directors, photographers, and dancers they have per capita.[10] The high-end of his index is both geographically concentrated in major urban areas and highly correlated to other concentrations - including higher education and a strong high-tech industry.

In a subsequent article, Florida and Gary Gates provide further evidence of the strong link between diversity, tolerance and high-technology growth.[11] Interestingly, they identify large urban concentrations of gays as the leading indicator of high-technology success, followed by the concentration of bohemians, proportion of foreign-born residents, and overall diversity. Major Canadian cities would rank very high on all of these measures.

Why do these factors matter in the new economy? Because people are the greatest resource for today's companies and most skilled employees increasingly value quality of life, diversity, and tolerance over other considerations when deciding where they wish to locate.

However, while Canada is recognized as a tolerant country and the level of diversity in our major cities is unparalleled, we are failing to "compete" with American cities with regard to investment in services, facilities, and infrastructure. In Toronto, provincial support for the arts has been hit harder than just about any other area of spending since the 1995 election of the Conservative Government of Mike Harris. The anti-arts agenda of the current government, during a period of great economic growth, does not contrast well with that of the Ontario NDP Government. Under Bob Rae, Ontario maintained high levels of cultural spending and subsidies during a punishing recession. What was missing, however, was the public recognition of the links between cultural activity and economic development.

In terms of infrastructural development, urban planner Joe Berridge points out that the national and state governments in the United States are heavily involved in subsidizing urban development. For example, Toronto is unique among major North American cities in that neither the provincial nor federal governments contribute a penny to our urban transit system. In the United States, the federal government alone would provide a city the size of Toronto with $42 million annually for transportation, $155 million per year for community economic development, and $47 million annually to support affordable housing.[12] Without state support, Toronto, like other Canadian cities, will be unable to make the environmental, lifestyle, transportation, cultural, and urban renewal investments necessary to compete in the new economy. As Berridge puts it, "we are in the odd situation in which our [US] competition has become interventionist, while we remain in a neo-conservative mindset, suspicious of any public expenditure."[13] Furthermore, this kind of direct support for cities - so critical in the global economy - seems to be immune to the trade-agreement-based challenges that constrain traditional economic policy debates.

For the NDP, the arguments above suggest that our opposition to massive tax cuts and the stultifying rhetoric about the brain drain has been misplaced. It is not only because quality public services and social equality are inherent goods that they should be protected. Rather, precisely because human beings *do* share our values, they seek communities that encourage human diversity and tolerance, sponsor the arts, support parks and recreation, offer clean air and clean water, value expanded educational opportunities, and that provide the quality public services that ensure that our streets are not crime-ridden and poverty-stricken. And it is the ability of urban areas to attract talented and trained citizens that will determine their success in the new economy.

THE NEW URBAN CHALLENGES

Throughout this chapter, I have suggested that we engage in

the debate about how to promote economic growth, encourage innovation, and increase our global competitiveness. Without a new commitment to economic matters the New Democratic Party will never regain its ability to speak out forcefully, with passion and credibility, about the social problems we face in Canada. While social inequality is not disappearing in our society, the Party's current marginalization means that we are increasingly useless to those on whose behalf we assume we speak. And we must regain our voice. The challenges are mounting in our cities and the emerging urban economy may very well exacerbate them unless we rise to the challenge of change.

In Toronto, the spatial division of social inequality is increasingly apparent between the city and its growing suburbs. In Canada, Ontario paid the highest price for the free trade agreements of the 1980s and 1990s. The impact was greatest in Toronto and the recovery here has been much slower than the experience of Toronto's suburbs.[14]

Average incomes are significantly lower in Toronto and the distribution of incomes reveals a larger gap between rich and poor than in surrounding cities. Poverty rates in Toronto have increased from 19% in 1991 to 28% in 1996, with the number of children living in low-income families increasing by 66% over the same period - 60,000 children (in 1998) depend on food banks to survive.[15] As in other growing cities, Toronto faces a large housing shortfall with vacancy rates approaching zero, no funding for social housing, and 200,000 tenants barely making their current rents.[16] These are challenges that can not be met by the market alone.

A related challenge is the increasing influence in our cities of the developers and privateers seeking to profit from public services. In many of our cities, progressive councillors, whether or not they are Party members, are leading the fight against untrammeled market-driven development. Their willingness to cooperate with the NDP depends on our ability to take the urban struggle to the provincial and federal levels.

The argument advanced in front of our local councils is not that different from that advanced in the fight against free trade and in more recent attempts by the federal Liberals to get out of the "business" of government. As William Tabb argues, "it is assumed that what is good for real-estate and other business interests will be best for the rest of the city's residents. After all, protecting and enhancing the tax base and promoting job creation is the key to wider prosperity and an ability to pay for social programs... Economic growth and greater efficiency will eventually be good for everyone and there is no alternative in any case."[17]

Tabb goes on to argue, however, that these arguments share with assaults on provincial and federal spending the oversight that market dynamics created many of the urban problems for which government intervention was originally demanded. The market - as an abstract concept - can not save our cities or our nation. In Toronto, the Ontario Government uses its appointees to the Ontario Municipal Board to overrule many attempts by local governments to mitigate the effects of change and to limit development. Without real powers and effective control over municipal issues, local democracy faces the real prospect of withering on the vine.

This being said, market forces are real and should not be ignored by the NDP or any other party that seeks to represent majority opinion. As I have argued above, many of *our* issues - like homelessness, spending on arts and culture, progressive taxation, rent control, and a living wage - are becoming key determinants of competitiveness for leading cities and nations.

However, the new economy also encourages economic disparities between the highly educated, high skill knowledge workers and the rest of society. As Manuel Castells argues, precisely because the knowledge economy, "concentrates wealth and power, while polarizing social groups according to their skills, unless deliberate policies correct the structural tendencies we are also witnessing the emergence of a social dualism that could ultimately lead to the formation of a dual city."[18]

Without effective political intervention, the Dual City will emerge from the tendency of the new economy to generate increasing disparities between those with skills at the top and those who serve them in service industries or are marginalized through unemployment. Another characteristic of the Dual City painfully evident in Canadian cities is the use of immigrant workers to fill less desirable jobs. A progressive approach to managing these changes would encompass job training, education, language training, immigrant settlement programs, acceptance of foreign educational credentials, housing supports, and income redistribution.

For Castells, the transformative power of new technologies creates a large political challenge for the left, to bridge the gap between the old economy and society and the new. As he puts it, the most important challenge for us is "the articulation of the globally-oriented economic functions of the city with the locally-rooted society and culture."[19] This is the new battleground for the New Democratic Party and one for which we are well prepared.

NDP VOTERS ARE URBAN VOTERS

Although working men and women from rural farms and small resource towns played a large role in the CCF, the political direction for the new party was heavily influenced by urban intellectuals. Today, despite some important pockets of support in rural Saskatchewan, Manitoba, Northern Ontario, and Atlantic Canada, our fortunes depend largely on the success of our candidates in the cities. The NDP is increasingly an urban party.

The contrast between town and country in terms of NDP support is stark. The NDP, simply put, can not survive without its urban base and the future of the party, in the medium term, will depend on our ability to translate core urban support into seats in the House of Commons.

Looking at the last federal election, there was a steady increase in NDP votes the closer one gets to our urban downtowns. In Halifax, the NDP vote was 11% over the provincial vote. Party support in Toronto's seven downtown ridings was more than twice that of our Ontario vote. In Saskatchewan and Manitoba, four of our five seats are in urban ridings. In Alberta, NDP support in Edmonton is almost double the provincial average. And finally, both of our two seats in British Columbia are in Vancouver.[20]

If the Party is to be rebuilt in the next election, the victories we need will come in Victoria, Vancouver, Edmonton, Saskatoon, Regina, Winnipeg, Hamilton, Windsor, Toronto, Kingston, Ottawa, Montreal, Halifax, and St. John's.

In many of these cities, progressive leaders - whether formally affiliated to the NDP or not - play important roles. Municipal politics - precisely because it *is* solution-oriented, rooted in local communities, and disconnected from traditional political loyalties - provides a healthy breeding ground for New Democrat politicians and their supporters. How many of us have encountered former activists who have turned from the estoteric and largely unsuccessful provincial and federal arenas to the immediate engagement of city hall? Electoral allies exist in most cities, a strong urban vision would allow us to encourage and engage in local political action and mobilization.

In Toronto, the Party's urban base is very important. We have a considerable number of sympathetic councillors at the local level and three strong representatives in the provincial legislature. However, in the last three elections we have been unable to translate this local support into a winning strategy at the federal level. While we have mobilized our base, we lack a message that appeals to the broader public and, lacking a strong national presence, we have failed to win seats in the House of Commons.

Despite the lack of a message for urban voters, support for the NDP is increasingly concentrated in the downtown core of Toronto. Recent research on provincial voting patterns in Ontario demonstrate this reality.[21] In 1975, the NDP vote in downtown Toronto - what was once, before forced amalgamation, the City of Toronto - was 5% above the provincial average. Fourteen years later, NDP support was almost 15% higher than the provincial average. With one exception, Liberal and Tory support in downtown Toronto has always been below their provincial levels of support. However, the ruling Tories have seen the Toronto "disadvantage" grow from -1% in 1975 to -5% in 1990 and a staggering -17% in the most recent provincial election in 1999.

The steep erosion in Tory support since Mike Harris' 1995 victory may explain a great deal of their antipathy to the concerns, lifestyles, and municipal affairs of Ontario's largest city. The Tories can not be faulted for identifying their regional friends and enemies. It seems clear that the Harris Government has given up on the nine ridings that make up the old city core, preferring instead to use their dominance of the 905 region and real strength in Toronto's former suburbs to hem in the electoral power of downtown Torontonians.

Today, our real opposition in the city of Toronto is the Liberal Party. The Liberals clearly have a much stronger base in Toronto than either the Tories or the New Democratic Party. This is painfully true at the federal level where the advantages of the Liberal Party over the right-wing parties and the NDP are almost too numerous to count. These include massive resources, strong support from many diverse communities, savvy (if unexciting) local MPs and extensive vertical links with provincial counterparts, munici-pal allies, and community activists. The Liberal machine in Toronto is indeed a formidable beast.

However, as I argued above, the Liberal tradition of hijacking our agenda may be limited by that Party's own past success. When you represent 101 of 103 Ontario ridings federally and must win back scores of suburban and rural ridings from the Conservatives to win provincially, your ability to campaign on an expressly urban platform is severely constrained.

TOWARDS A NEW URBAN VISION

To succeed in the 21st century, the NDP must combine its well-established opposition to social inequality with a renewed - or per-haps, rediscovered - understanding and engagement with economic issues. I have argued that Canada's cities provide an excellent arena for this progressive vision and one that should favour the New Democratic Party. Recent literature on localism and the new economy suggests that our social democratic agenda can be fruit-fully combined with a strong urban agenda.

Any urban platform that we do develop as a Party must, of course, be done in close consultation with local activists. The pa-rameters of the platform and vision can and should be adopted to different cities in different regions. However, here are some elements that could be included:[22]

- An emphasis on the downtown as symbolic and cultural heart of our cities, conservation of heritage properties, support for innovative urban design and architecture
- Support for compact urban development and the reclama-tion of abandoned industrial sites
- Support for main street businesses on economic and diver-sity grounds as well as to help preserve existing cultural com-munity identities
- Funding for accessible and affordable public transit to re-duce reliance on car travel within and between cities
- Support for the arts, in all forms from the mainstream to emerging arts to "elite" cultural expression
- Providing public infrastructure and other investment to

leverage private and community investment

• Funding for environmental retrofitting of buildings, waste and pollution reduction, and energy efficiency

• Funding of immigrant settlement and language training programs along with measures to increase the recognition of credentials and training received overseas

• Stewardship and subsidization of the costs involved in connecting innovative small companies with sources of venture capital

• Efforts to build regional innovation networks in partnership with educational institutions, businesses, unions, and unorganized workers

• Strong support for affordable public housing to relieve the homelessness crisis

• And property tax reform to ensure that taxes support public services without pricing businesses and low-income families out of the city

If the New Democratic Party rises to meet the challenges our cities face, it can reconnect once again with the Canadian public. Most New Democrats cherish their party because of its contribution, over many years, to public debate. If we all engage in the process of developing new approaches to new problems, we can construct the foundations of a new progressive left. Urban policy, rather than a footnote to the federal platform, should be a major theme for the New Democratic Party, at all levels, as it goes through its process of rejuvenation.

---

[1]Manuel Castells, "European Cities, the Informational Society, and the Global Economy," *New Left Review* 204 (March/April 1994).

[2]Joel Kotkin and Ross C. DeVol, "Knowledge-Value Cities in the Digital Age," Milken Institute, February 2001, page 23.

[3]David Lewis, *The Good Fight*. Toronto: MacMillan of Canada, 1981, page 291.

[4]City of Toronto, *Toronto Competes: An Assessment of Toronto's Global Competitiveness*, February 2000, page 4.

[5]Meric S. Gertler, "Urban Economy and Society in Canada: Flows of People, Capital and Ideas," *Isuma: Canadian Journal of Policy Research*, Volume

2, Number 3, Autumn 2001, page 125.

[6]Cited in Richard Florida, "The Geography of Bohemia," unpublished paper, Carnegie Mellon University, January 2001.

[7]Cited in Jane Jacobs, *Cities and the Wealth of Nations*, New York: First Vintage Books, 1985, page 223.

[8]Manuel Castells, "European Cities, the Informational Society, and the Global Economy," *New Left Review* 204 (March/April 1994), page 20.

[9]Kotkin and DeVol, page 13.

[10]Florida, Richard, "The Geography of Talent," unpublished paper, January 2001.

[11]Richard Florida and Gary Gates, "Technology and Tolerance: The Importance of Diversity to High-Technology Growth," The Bookings Institution, June 2001.

[12]Joe Berridge, "Shaping Toronto's Future," Forum sponsored by the City of Toronto, April 7, 1999.

[13]Ibid.

[14]"Toronto Competes," page 19.

[15]Ibid., page 26, 27.

[16]Op Cit.

[17]William K. Tabb, "Privatization and Urban Issues: A Global Perspective," *Monthly Review*. Volume 52, Number 9, February 2001, page 36.

[18]Castells, pages 28 to 30.

[19]Castells, page 30

[20]Elections Canada, *2000 Election Results*, available online at www.elections.ca.

[21]The following figures draw on unpublished research by Doug Hamilton, Information Officer with the Ontario New Democratic Party Caucus. While provincial results for the NDP have traditionally been somewhat higher than federal voting results, they generally follow the same pattern.

[22]I would like to thank Fred Gloger, urban issues researcher for the Ontario New Democratic Party caucus, for providing many of these ideas.

Reforming Political Finance

ROBERT MACDERMID

How political parties and campaigns are financed is not a top of the mind issue for most Canadians. Television news and newspapers rarely mention the issue. The fact that the mainstream media are regulated by the state, that many media corporations are large contributors to political parties, and that federal and provincial states and parties are major media advertisers may have something to do with this reticence. Given these mutually advantageous relations, it is not surprising that commentary is sporadic. But there are signs that party finance reform might draw attention and support. The Manitoba NDP have recently rewritten the province's party finance rules, the rise and demise of the Canadian Alliance is sometimes discussed in terms of its financial backers, provincial party funding scandals are a regular occurrence and, US campaign finance reform is always being discussed, if seldom enacted.

A party financing reform debate raises important democratic principles that citizens can easily recognize. Secret contributions to parties, the wealthy being permitted to make huge contributions, large foreign-owned corporations contributing to Canadian parties, policy outcomes that favour contributors and the relationship between economic power and political power are all principles with a great deal of resonance. Such a debate provides the opportunity to demonstrate to voters the relationship between corporate interests and parties that support a corporate agenda and are financed by those same corporations. These are policy positions and principles that left-leaning voters and those concerned about globalization expect the NDP to advance. The slowness of the party to lead discussions of democratic reforms has allowed the Reform and Alliance parties to take up some of these positions. But on party funding, the now increasingly corporate-backed Alliance party is very vulnerable to arguments in support of democratic reforms.

WHAT DO CANADIANS THINK ABOUT PARTY AND CAMPAIGN FINANCING ISSUES?

When asked about party and campaign finance issues, Canadians display a strong degree of democratic fairness and an awareness of the relationship between the wealth and politics that suggests they would support systems and regulations that are quite different from those now in place. For example, 88 percent of a sample of Canadians taken in the spring of 2000 agreed with the proposition that "people with money have a lot of influence over government."[1] A 1990 survey found that 43 percent agreed with the statement that "anybody who gives money to a political party expects something in return."[2] Thirty-six percent of the 1990 sample agreed with the statement that "the party that spends the most during an election is almost sure to win the election," but by 2000, that figure had grown to 60 percent.[3] The 1990 survey also found that 88 percent of respondents thought that there should be limits on how much money the parties can spend during campaigns,[4] 59 percent thought that there should be a ceilings on how much money anyone can give to a party,[5] and 79 percent supported disclosure of the identity of contributors.[6] On the evidence of survey questions across about 35 years, it is fair to say that Canadians are about equally divided on whether corporations and trade unions should be able to give money to parties,[7] but "ninety-one percent of those who believe that corporations and unions should have the right to contribute also support the idea of requiring these groups to obtain approval from their shareholders or members."[8]

Canadians' growing concern about the role of money in politics runs parallel to their growing sense of political cynicism. Over the past thirty years, the percentage of respondents believing that governments don't care about them, or that elected members soon lose touch with their constituents, or do not trust government or believe that the people running government are crooked, has been steadily rising.[9]

While the evidence of public opinion about party financing needs to be treated carefully in the absence of a public debate and because it its limited to a few surveys, there is enough of it to suggest that Canadians would support tighter restrictions on party financing. Quebec has had such a funding regime for almost 25 years and Manitoba instituted similar reforms in the past year. It is worth looking at those experiences more closely.

MONEY AND PARTIES IN QUEBEC PROVINCIAL POLITICS

So unique and popular are the funding rules governing Quebec provincial parties, that the federal Bloc Quebecois party *voluntarily* followed parts of the provincial rules on contributions between 1993 and 2000. Since the Quiet Revolution of the 1960s, Quebec has been a leader in campaign and party finance reform borrowing ideas from other jurisdictions and developing unique elements that have been copied in other provinces and countries. Quebec's reforms were begun in 1963 by the Liberal government and continued by the first Parti Quebecois administration and have remained largely unaltered through subsequent Liberal and PQ administrations. The Quebec system, sometimes called "grassroots party financing" or "financement populaire," has a number of key features that are present in other systems, but combines these in a manner that is unique to Canada. Quebec was the first Canadian jurisdiction to adopt the British practice of official agents who are responsible for a candidate's fund-raising and spending and required these agents to file reports on expenditures as well limiting what could be spent during the election period. The 1963 reforms also introduced state funding in the form of reimbursement of a portion of campaign expenses for candidates gaining at least 20% of the vote. Perhaps the most important innovation was the requirement for central parties to comply with the same reporting requirements as candidate campaigns and placed a limit on their now declared expenditures. While no state funding for central parties was provided in 1963, the Bourrassa Liberal government amended the law in 1975 to provide an allowance for parties that is divided according to the number of votes won by each party at the previous election. In 2000, that allowance gave to both the Liberal and PQ just over $1.1 million. Action Démocratique du Québec received just over $315,000 and no other party received more than $18,000. In the case of both the Liberal and PQ parties, the public money made up about 21% of both parties revenues, the Liberals raising $5.9 million and the PQ raising $5.6 million. The Parti Quebecois put in place the final elements of the province's unique system. In 1977, it adopted Ontario's then newly implemented system of requiring central parties and constituency organizations to file annual reports on revenues and expenditures and these plus the candidates to file reports for campaign periods. It also adopted the then recent federal requirement that the identities of donors contributing more than $200 be disclosed. The 1977 changes also adopted a tax credit for small donations, an idea first tried by the Canadian government. The two most controversial changes were a cap on contributions of $3,000 and a ban on corporate and trade union contributions.[10]

Some have argued that Quebec's grassroots financing system results in governing parties that are flush with cash and an opposition party with very little.[11] Liberal and PQ revenues did fluctuate considerably throughout the eighties and nineties and generally reflected the popularity of the party. Part of this fluctuation was the result of the Liberal party success at fund-raising events during the late nineteen-eighties, a practice condemned by the PQ as selling access to cabinet ministers. Others have seen these fluctuations in revenue as the equivalent of price signals in a market telling parties that they need to develop policies or change leaders and images. At a minimum, the need to collect money from individuals means that parties have to pay attention to their members and develop a broader membership and support base. Even the Liberals, who generally focus on events that allow contributors to get access to ministers, still have to arrange an enormous number of these events, (over 200 in 2000 as compared to the 22 fund-raising events organized by the Ontario Progressive Conservative party in the same year) and with high ticket prices and a low ceiling on total contributions, repeat

but not necessarily a home or place of business address. At both the federal level and in Ontario, when lists of contributors are posted to websites, the way most people encounter the information, addresses are stripped from the lists in order to keep the lists out of the hands of marketers. US rules require names, amounts and home addresses in addition to occupation and employer. All of the information is posted to the web[14] and commercial list hunters are kept at bay by heavy fines and the salting of the lists with a number of bogus names and addresses, which if they receive junk mail, will alert officials to improper uses of the disclosed lists. Undoubtedly there is some illegal use of the disclosed information, but it is well worth the extra transparency.

Disclosure never seems so important as when one learns about systems where party financial transactions are completely secret. The Labour government in Britain has only this year moved to reform archaic finance laws that in January of 2001, allowed Labour to accept 3 contributions of over £2 million each in complete secrecy that only accidentally became public.[15] The UK Conservatives are said to be even more heavily dependent on one former Belize businessman.

WHO SHOULD BE PERMITTED TO CONTRIBUTE?

In most provincial jurisdictions and at the federal level, parties may take contributions from individuals who are Canadian citizens or permanent residents and who make contributions out of their own resources. All rules prohibit contributors from passing along funds given to them by someone else. This undoubtedly takes place but under current rules is very difficult to discover and police. In most jurisdictions other than Quebec and Manitoba, parties may also accept money from all corporations including non-profit publicly owned corporations such as universities, hospitals, municipalities and school boards with the one exception of charitable corporations. There is usually a requirement that the corporation be actively carrying on business in the jurisdiction, thus preventing a company from setting up a subsidiary for the sole purposes of making contributions or for masking the source of those donations. Finally, trade unions are permitted to make contributions, but usually only if they represent workers within the jurisdiction.

Even in those nations where parties are heavily financed by

the state, individuals are permitted to contribute and it is certainly desirable on democratic grounds that citizens who stand for office, vote for parties, work for them and believe in them, should be allowed to support them either through labour or modest monetary contributions. But corporations and trade unions do not vote, cannot run for office, cannot constitute a political party and so it can be argued, should not have the same right as citizens to be active in the political process.

The suggestion of a ban on corporate contributions usually brings howls from the parties that "live" on money from businesses and from the business community as well, because their investments in parties are ways of influencing general government policy and specific decisions. But there are good reasons for such a ban. We have examples of systems that work without money from businesses, Quebec politics has shown that parties can survive without corporate or trade union money and produce broadly supported and democratic political movements. And Quebec is not the only example. Candidates for the US Congress may only accept donations from individuals, corporate and trade union donations are not permitted. Of course corporations, trade unions and American parties have connived to get around these rules through the use of PACs, political action committees, that are often set up and solely funded by corporations.

There are other good reasons for banning corporate contributions to parties. Democratic equality is based on the perhaps utopian notion of equal political power through limiting every person to a single vote. If only individual citizens can contribute and there are realistic limits on the size of contributions, then the economic inequalities present in market societies cannot be translated into political power. The large corporations that provide the bulk of corporate funding to parties have great wealth and power that is commanded by a small number of very wealthy citizens who can direct not just their own wealth in the purpose of political ends, but the considerable wealth of the corporation and its subsidiaries as well. Allowing corporations to give to parties therefore allows individuals to give more than once, and to translate economic inequalities into political inequalities. Even libertarians support a ban on contributions from trade unions and publicly-traded corporations arguing that union dues or profits that belong to members or shareholders are being used to support the political views of leadership or management.

The are also practical reasons for banning corporate contributions. Corporate organization challenges even the most comprehensive disclosure and contributor rules. Large corporations have national homes of convenience and have colonized almost every nation with subsidiaries. As I have mentioned, even to limit corporate contributors to those carrying on business in Canada is not enough to rule out money from trans-national firms that may have political goals at odds with most Canadians. What is best for Glaxo Wellcome, long running drug patents and high drug prices, may not be best for most Canadians.

In party finance systems with limits on the size of contributions, as is the case in Ontario, caps can be flaunted through having multiple subsidiaries make contributions. Peter Munk's control of Barrick Gold and TrizecHahn have permitted him to direct those and 28 other companies to contribute $721,000 to the Progressive Conservative party of Ontario between 1995 and 2000.[16] Munk, his wife and directors and senior managers have given another $58,000 to the party. This is not an isolated example, residential developers have similar contribution patterns. And imagine how easy it would be even under a capped contribution system if Brascan, owned by Edward and Peter Bronfman, decided to "buy" a political party by contributing through many of its more than 350 partly or wholly controlled companies.

Even though there is no contribution limit at the federal level, companies still give through multiple wholly and partly owned subsidiaries. Some person at SNC Lavalin, a large engineering firm, directed 15 wholly owned subsidiaries to give a total of $728,000 to the Liberal party of Canada between 1997 and 2000. Voters have a right to know that this is the game, but it is not always easy to determine who owns or controls companies making disclosure meaningless. The ownership of private corporations is private, unknown to all of us but Revenue Canada. The recent change to federal legislation to require the names of a director of a numbered company does not really address the important questions of who is directing the wealth of the company to support a political party. Knowing a company's name is not enough, we should be able to know which citizen is wielding this power and why they are doing so.

Finally, corporate money does not go equally to all political parties, but supports parties and governments that favour business interests over others. While business leaders and politicians will often claim that corporate contributions are motivated by a philanthropic concern to support democratic regimes, the pattern of their giving is much more like a pattern of investment in political parties that support the interest of business.[17] Of all the contributions flowing into Ontario's provincial political parties, about 45 percent comes from corporations, but in every year since 1996, more than 80% of those corporate contributions have flowed to the Mike Harris Progressive Conservative party. The Liberal party of Canada has scooped up about 65% of corporate money in every year between 1994 and 1999, with the remainder being divided between the Progressive Conservative and the Reform/Alliance parties.

CONTRIBUTION LIMITS

Limiting the size of a contribution directly limits the amount of influence a donor can exercise through the party and campaign finance system. The more a contributor gives to a party, the more they are likely to be listened to, and given privileged access to decision makers. Party fund-raising builds this logic into event ticket sales, charging the highest prices for small exclusive events or seating at head tables and with cabinet ministers or premiers, prime ministers and party leaders. This selling of access whether effective for the buyer or not, fosters the impression that democratic governments serve only their own supporters, who are the wealthy ones able to purchase access.

There is no cap on donation size at the federal level in Canada. This has led to a number of very large union, corporate and individual contributions to parties. Between 1997 and 1999, the federal Liberals took in 448 donations in excess of $10,000 from businesses. By contrast, just 11 individuals gave greater than that amount and just 4.7% of all the 43,313 individual donations greater than $100 to the party in that period were greater than $500. The 1999 Ontario contribution caps allowed individuals to give up to $25,000 to a central party and candidates and constituency organizations. In that year, about 15,400 individuals[18] made total contributions in excess of $100 to the Progressive Conservative party, but just 135 of them (less than 1 per cent) gave a total of $3,000 or more and less than 8 per cent of contributors gave more than a total of $1,000 over the several contribution periods.

Contribution limits mean almost nothing to 99% of donors who give far less than the maximums in jurisdictions where upper limits exist. Limits above $2,000 or $3,000 do nothing but license the wealthy to give more and thereby exercise influence. Higher limits also ensure that parties will seek out these wealthy donors because the logic and economics of raising funds dictates that they go in search of large donors.

While Quebec and Manitoba have set a cap at $3,000, that is still far above the median contribution. There are precedents for even lower limits. Candidates for the US Congress cannot accept contributions from individuals (trade union and corporate contributions are not permitted) larger than $1,000. Money does flow into candidate campaigns from other directions, from political action Committees and other party committees, but the original intent of the legislation was to set a low limit. The lower the limit, the less the appearance of influence and the more individuals who will be able to give the limit making access widespread and ensuring that the voices being heard are broadly representative. The lower limit also forces parties to concentrate their fund-raising efforts on smaller contributors, meaning that they will have to, on occasion, listen to the needs and wants of those who are not amongst the wealthiest.

CONTROLLING EXPENDITURE

Reforms on the revenue side only make sense if there are effective controls on how much parties can spend. Party campaign and annual real expenditures have been climbing in the past decade, largely driven by the costs and preference for campaign television advertising as a primary method for communicating with voters. American studies have suggested that negative advertising disgusts some voters enough to keep them from voting. And we all have to wonder if TV advertising techniques and 15 second spots are the best way to discuss important policy issues.

A limit on TV advertising or even the requirement that both public and private broadcasters make free time available to the parties during elections is not unreasonable. Private broadcasters have a license to use the public airwaves, and the requirement to provide

213

free political time is entirely reasonable. Providing more free time to parties would mean that they would have to raise less money to purchase air-time.

Both the federal and Ontario systems claim to have strict expenditure controls but these are more illusion than reality. More and more expenditure categories are removed from under election period spending caps and major expenditures that any citizen would surely classify as election related are now removed from under the cap. For example, both federal and Ontario parties need not include campaign opinion polling as a campaign expense. In addition, major television advertising expenditures now take place before the campaign starts and are almost completely uncontrolled. The Manitoba reforms have led the way in controlling pre-election campaign expenditures. This trend saw the Ontario Progressive Conservatives spend almost as much money on TV advertising in the month before they called the 1999 election, as they spend during the expenditure-capped campaign period.[19] These kinds of practices make expenditure caps almost irrelevant.

PUBLIC SUBSIDIES

Public subsidies, that is money from government tax revenues, flow to parties in the form of tax credits for contributions, the deduction of a portion of a contribution from tax owing, in the form of direct subsidies to candidates and parties for a portion of campaign expenditures or, as in Quebec, as an annual subsidy to the parties. Federal rules and those of every province now provide at least one of these types of subsidies to parties, though the level of support varies across jurisdictions.[20] Exact figures are difficult to arrive at since the total value of the tax credits is sometimes not publicly available. Quebec's system of annual allowances provides money to parties in between elections and generally keeps the parties out of the crippling debt positions that can keep parties from being competitive in high cost elections. Public subsidies in Germany and Sweden in the nineteen eighties made up over 70% of total income for national party headquarters.[21]

A discussion of increased public subsidies is sure to draw criticism from the right, although the finances of those parties and of the think tanks that support them are also reliant on tax credits, public funding and charitable donations, so any arguments they might make are surely compromised. There are many difficult issues, such as a formula for division, the level of funding and so on, but all of these problems have been addressed in other countries.[22] Some level of public funding allows parties a secure and basic operating budget and partially frees them from the work of raising funds. Under the current regulations, most parties dedicate more time and resources to fund-raising than to any other activity. Do we want political parties to be principally fund-raising organizations?

CONCLUSION

Reforming the rules that govern the financing of political parties can create parties that are more attentive to the voters they must rely on for funding. The broader the base of that funding and the lower the contribution limit, the more all parties must rely on donations from voters of average means. And parties and politicians who must raise money from a large number of individuals are more likely to reflect the needs of the voters they will meet at fund-raising functions. Since party funding became more public in the nineteenseventies, the Conservative and Liberal parties at both provincial and federal levels have been heavily dependent on funding from businesses, so it not surprising that the policies of those parties should reflect the pro-business attitudes of their major financial backers.

Introducing or reducing contribution limits, controlling expenses and increasing public funding should reduce the need for parties to raise large sums of money. If they need less money because they cannot spend it, then perhaps parties can become the sites of the kind of democratic policy discussion that many have supposed that they should be.

[1]Paul Howe and David Northrup, "Strengthening Canadian Democracy," Policy Matters, Vol l. No. 5, July 2000. (Montreal, Institute for Research in Public Policy, 2000), 37.
[2]André Blais and Elisabeth Gidengil, Making Representative Democracy Work. The Views of Canadians. (Toronto, Dundurn Press, 1991), 46.
[3]Howe and Northrup, 38.
[4]Blais and Gidengil, 84,85.
[5]Blais and Gidengil, 93, 96.
[6]Blais and Gidengil, 94.

[7]Blais and Gidengil, 99.
[8]Blais and Gidengil, 102.
[9]Blais and Gidengil, 38; Howe and Northrup, 9.
[10]Massicotte, Louis, "Party Financing in Quebec: An Analysis of the Financial Reports of Parties, 1977-89" in F. Leslie Seidle ed., Provincial Party and Election Finance in Canada, (Toronto, Dundurn Press, 1990).
[11]Harold M Angell, Quebec's Party Financing System since 1978: Does it Work? Paper presented at the Annual General Meeting of the Canadian Political Science Association, Ottawa, June 8, 1993.
[12]David Roberts, "Manitoba to restrict donations," Globe and Mail, Wednesday, June 21, 2000.
[13]Blais and Gidengil, 93, 96
[14]http://www.fec.gov/
[15]"Cash for Labour," The Economist, January 4, 2001.
[16]Robert MacDermid, Funding the Common Sense Revolutionaries: Contributions to the Progressive Conservative Party of Ontario, 1995-97. (Toronto, Centre for Social Justice, 1999).
[17]Robert MacDermid, "Toward an Investment Theory of Canadian Electoral Politics," a paper presented at the Annual General Meetings of the Canadian Political Science Association, Quebec City, 2001.
[18]It is hard to be precise about this number since lists of contributors have spelling mistakes, sometimes include middle initials, and lists posted to the web never include addresses that would help match contributors across the 4 disclosed lists in Ontario for 1999.
[19]Robert MacDermid, "Changing Electoral Politics in Ontario: The 1999 Provincial Election," a paper presented at the Annual General Meetings of the Canadian Political Science Association, Quebec City, 2000.
[20]See: Peter P. Constantinou, "Public Funding of Political Parties, Candidates and Elections in Canada, in Leslie Seidle, ed., Issues in Party and Election Finance in Canada, (Toronto, Dundurn, 1991) and; Donald E. Blake, "Electoral Democracy in the Provinces," Montreal, Institute for Research in Public Policy, 2001.
[21]Arthur B. Gunlicks, ed. Campaign and Party Finance in North America and Western Europe, (Boulder, Col., Westview Press, 1993) p. 257.
[22]See Jane Jenson, "Innovation and Equity: the Impact of Public Funding," in Leslie Seidle, ed., Comparative Issues in Party and Election Finance, (Toronto, Dundurn, 1991).

VERA BRACKEN LIBRARY

3 3440 00178 370 2

MEDICINE HAT COLLEGE

JL 197 N4 B47 2001
What's left? : the New
Democratic Party in renewal

MAR 3   2003

DATE DUE		
APR 2 3 2003		
APR 1 7 2004		
MAR 2 3 2006		
APR 2 1 2008		
APR 1 5 2009		
DEC - 3 2009		
MAR 1 7 2010		
APR - 9 2010		
APR 2 6 2011		

AGMV Marquis

MEMBER OF SCABRINI MEDIA

Quebec, Canada
2001